# SENDO-RYU KARATE-DO

先道流空手道

# SENDO-RYU KARATE-DO

## The Way of Initiative

by
Professor Emeric Arus - 10th Dan

Turtle Press          Santa Fe

To contact the author: 0011-718-204-7523, www.sendo-ryu.com or stickyhandsjj@gmail.com

To order additional copies of this book, call 1-800-778-8785 or visit www.turtlepress.com

Illustrations by: Emeric Arus
Photographs by: George deLucenay Leon
Cover photo: Miklos Magyarosy and Jozsef Szakacs
Edited by: Christopher Hendry

ISBN 978-1-934903-10-0
LCCN  2008043537
Printed in the United States of America
Second edition

The author's intention in capitalizing the first letter of each word in Japanese, Chinese and Korean is to place emphasis on the words, contrary to grammatical rules. Throughout this book, "he" is used to refer to instructors, students and people. This is for ease of reading only and should be taken to mean he or she where appropriate.

10 9 8 7 6 5 4 3 2 1 0

**Warning-Disclaimer**

This book is designed to provide information on specific skills used in the martial art of Sendo-ryu Karate-do. It is not the purpose of this book to reprint all the information that is otherwise available to the author, publisher, printer or distributors. Anyone practicing the skills presented in this book should be physically capable to do so and have the permission of a licensed physician before participating in this activity or any physical activity. Every effort has been made to make this book as complete and accurate as possible. However, there may be mistakes, both typographical and in content. Therefore, this text should be used only as a general guide and not the ultimate source of information on the subjects presented here in this book on sambo or any skill or subject. The purpose of this book is to provide information. The author, publisher, printer and distributors shall neither have liability nor responsibility to any person or entity with respect to loss or damages caused, or alleged to have been caused, directly or indirectly, by the information contained in this book.

**Library of Congress Cataloguing in Publication Data**

Arus, Emeric.
  Sendo-ryu karate-do / by Emeric Arus.
     p. cm.
  Includes index.
  ISBN 978-1-934903-10-0
  1. Karate. I. Title.
GV1114.3.A777 2008
796.815'3--dc22
                          2008043537

# Contents

# Disclaimer

The publisher of this instructional book WILL NOT BE HELD RESPONSIBLE in any way whatsoever for any physical injury, or damage of any sort, that may occur as a result of reading and/or following the instructions given herein. It is essential, therefore, before attempting any of the physical activities described or depicted in this book, the reader(s) should consult a qualified physician to ascertain whether the reader(s) should engage in the physical activity described or depicted in this book.

As the physical activities described, or depicted herein, may be overly taxing or sophisticated for the reader(s), it is essential that this advice be followed and a physician consulted.

# Dedication & Acknowledgements

I would like to dedicate this book to my loving son, who helped me and served as the Uke in the pictures of this book and to my wife, who always supported me to finish this book. Also, I would like to dedicate this book to all Romanian Karateka (instructors and students) who started Karate with me in the late sixties.

A special appreciation to my very good friend, student of fencing, George deLucenay Leon. A true gentleman who took all the pictures for this book and who also advised me how to set up this book.

A special appreciation to my best student/instructor Dr. Attila A. Czegeni 6th Dan President of the Hungarian Sendo-Ryu Karatedo Federation for his loyalty and dedication to Sendo-Ryu.

# Foreword

There is no such thing as a bible of Karate technique in a sense of one authoritative statement to the teachings of all Karate methodology. And for this there are several reasons. First, due to the political standings of Karate today, there is no one recognized authority that can supervise all Karate systems and methodology that would be agreed upon by the majority of practitioners. Second, because of the wide range of beliefs, technical differences, countries, etc., it would make such a volume impossible to compile. Therefore, bulk of the knowledge of Karate is held within specialized manuals that expound upon the technical differences of Kata (formal exercise) and Waza (technique) handed down to us by various founders. There are, of course, the standard so-called Karate bibles. Mas Oyama's *This is Karate*, Gichin Funakoshi's, *Karate-do Kyohan* are some of the better known. Yet each of these books deals more with the actual technical movements of an individual system rather than the general theories behind the movements.

Our western knowledge of Karate is not yet one hundred years old. First came sporadic translations of Karate texts that were questionable in theory, content and authenticity; then the west was treated to translations of actual classic Karate volumes. Third came the myriad of volumes of the various Karate systems of Shotokan, Goju-Ryu, Shito-Ryu, Wado-Ryu, etc.

The first attempt at an anthology to draw from and the whole field was made in the 1960s, and these attempts were more dictionaries attempting to define various Karate terminologies as they apply to techniques. The one thing all of these books have in common is that they are aimed at the person with an extreme amount of previous knowledge in the field or with some type of scholarly Karate knowledge.

The average laymen attempting to pick up these books would find them very difficult to comprehend. The need for a book written in simple, clear-cut language has been a necessity for many years. This volume allots the right proportions of space to the various techniques of Karate, its theories, methodology, its histories. The major portion of this text deals with the actual execution of these techniques aimed not at learning how to theoretically beat an opponent but instead offers solid, sound advice on the actual applications.

It has been indeed a pleasure to go through this script for the *Sendo-Ryu* Karate volume by Professor Emeric Arus. This book is a fine product of eastern thoughts and western minds. The explanations are direct and precise. I am sure that those who read the book will gain an immediate insight into Karate, and will enjoy the nectar of health in body, contentment of mind, and spiritual satisfaction.

Karate is an immortal art, science and philosophy. It is the best subjective look at the psycho-anatomy of mankind ever conceived for the experience of physical, mental, intellectual and spiritual well-being. It has stood the test of time, from the beginning of Oriental civilization, and it will remain supreme, as a precise psycho-physical science, for centuries to come.

There are many different types of cells in the body with physical, psychological, emotional, intellectual, and spiritual functions. It is known that each cell has a life of its own. These cells are the pearls of life. In the practice of Karate, every cell is consciously made to absorb the copulas supply of fresh blood and energy thus satisfying the embodied soul.

With serenity one then experiences self by the self and rests the self in the lap of the soul. This is why the master calls Karate a Way of Life.

I am pleased to be associated with this book by my dear friend Emeric Arus. My suggestions have been incorporated in the book and I will be glad if those who read it appreciate and practice the art of Karate. Emeric and I have been travelers, each of us seeking the answers to the Karate riddle. Each of us have taken different paths. Emeric's Karate began in the area of the world where there were no available teachers. Emeric was forced to learn Karate on his own through books and literature that he was able to procure. Because of many volumes written on Shotokan Karate, Emeric first began looking at the various Shotokan Karate manuals, learning how to perfect the Shotokan techniques, as found in the many books on the subject. After a sixteen years study of Shotokan, he was able to learn other style as Wado-Ryu about eight years. Yet to Professor Emeric Arus each of these styles of Karate was missing something.

Like many of the founders of old, Professor Arus took it upon himself to improve on these styles, generally being criticized by the traditional sect of Karate saying that there is "... no need to improve it. What is needed is a better understanding of the Karate in the first place." But Professor Arus continued to feel something was lacking and, from his lifelong dream, sprung forth *Sendo-Ryu*.

This book is his lifelong ambition to bring his message of Karate to the western world. Traditionalists will not agree; eclectic stylists will call it too rigid; and those in-between will find Professor Arus' book on Karate refreshing and insightful. In the end we are all but travelers, and I am reminded of a Buddhist poem:

> *The traveler owes the grateful scent*
> *of sweetness near he knows not went*
> *and pausing takes with forehead bare*
> *the benediction of the air.*

**George R. Parulski, Jr., Ph.D., Bs.D. - 8th Dan Hanshi**
**Vice President of Dai Nippon Seibukan Budo/Bugei Kai, Japan**
**USA Director / Okazaki Ha Shin Tenshin Shin'yo Bu Jutsu Renmei**

**January, 2000**

# Preface

In the last two to three decades, Karate, the art of empty hand fighting, has become very popular as a sport, as self-defense and as martial art.  Hundreds of books have been written about Kung-Fu, Taekwondo and Japanese styles, such as Shotokan, Goju-Ryu, Kyokushinkai, Uechi-Ryu, Shorin-Ryu, Kempo etc.  This, however, is the first book about Sendo-Ryu.

This book has been written for those Karateka, instructors who are interested in a comprehensive Karate book, for those who seek a proficient self-defense method, and for those practicing Sendo-Ryu, because it contains the majority of the mandatory technical requirements for belt advancement.

Sendo-Ryu Karatedo, which is a highly dynamic American-Japanese style, is based on scientific research conducted in four major Japanes styles:  Shotokan, Wado-Ryu, Goju-Ryu and Shito-Ryu Karatedo.  This is an American style because the founder is an American, but it is also a Japanese style because the roots and many of the techniques and much of the terminology is Japanese.  In Sendo-Ryu Karate, basic sparring, prearranged and semi-free sparring, are absolutely mandatory for belt advancement.  These technical skills and fighting requirements are arranged methodically and logically for learning and teaching purposes.

*Sendo* means the *way of initiative*, referring to defensive tactics that can be used in two ways:

1.  Stopping the opponent(s) attacks by attacking him first.  In this type of defensive tactics, using the *"SEN"* (initiative), defined as executing a move before the opponent's attack, can also be understood as two attacks executed simultaneously.  The one that is finalized first has the *"SEN."*

2.  Creating an opening on one's body with a large movement thereby giving an intentional target to the attacker, making it easier for the defender to defend (block) and counter.  This tactics is known as *2nd intention defense.*

A unique feature of this book that has never been seen before in any other Karate book is *IPPON KUMITE* - one step, one attack sparring, used *only* for self-defense purposes.  This fighting method teaches the student techniques such as:  Blocking, throwing, sweeping and grabbing the opponent's arm or leg.  The combat positions are natural, high and relaxed.

In *Ippon Kumite*, defense is based on the attacker's principle of *IKKEN HISATSU* (to kill or knock down with one blow).  This means that on a first attack there must be a definitive block and counter attack that makes it impossible for the attacker to continue his attack with follow-up techniques.  Based on this theory, the defender should throw or sweep his attacker because any off-balancing technique minimizes the attacker's opportunity to continue his attack.

If you have read enough books written about Shotokan, Goju Ryu, Kyokushinkai or any other style (except Wado-Ryu), you can see that there is a big difference in the way basic or prearranged sparring is set up, even as the essence of the styles are the same.

In Sendo-Ryu, however, one cannot break away from the mandatory rules of techniques and must follow the established path of the Sendo-Ryu Karatedo Federation.  This means that you are a traditionalist and have the best Budo (military way) spirit, because the exercises in Sendo-Ryu are related to the true martial way.

The content of the book is organized using Roman numerals for chapters and Arabic numerals for subchapters for easier understanding. This book is comprehensive because it contains history, philosophy, theory, training (basic and fighting techniques), methodology, injuries and treatments, Karate for children and the use of Karate equipment.

Sendo-Ryu is strongly connected to Jujutsu, Aikido, Aikijujutsu, Judo and knife fighting techniques, thus for the black belt test the Karateka must demonstrate his proficiency in disarming knife attacks.

Another unique feature of Sendo-Ryu Karatedo is its knife Kata, which is not required, or even known, in most Karate styles. The Tanto Kata (formal knife exercises) teaches attacks with stabbing, slashing, feints in different angles and defenses that are simple with detailed explanations.

Chapter III explains Karate training methods never before seen in any other Karate book, working periods for top athletes, sport calendar programming and division of effort in training.

Professor Arus has a background as a fencer with over 45 years of experience. He has been an Olympic fencer from Romania. The interest in Karate started at 30 years of age practicing Shotokan Karate constantly for approximately 16 years and an additional 8 years in Wado-Ryu Karate. After many years of practicing Karate, researching, reading over 600 books, magazines and articles and participating at scientific symposiums, Professor Arus has reached a conclusion: All styles have strong (good) and weak points.

This style tends to be very economical and effective and not only does it extract the best aspects of the 4 major Japanese styles mentioned above, but it also eliminates the weaker aspects of those particular styles. In addition, the author introduces new systematized fighting principles and teaching methodologies along with new improved Karate techniques.

The descriptions and explanations about blocking techniques are also unique to this book. In this style, arm blocking techniques are more like parrying techniques, than blocking by the use of hitting power, as in most other Karate styles. The reader will find detailed explanations and diagrams of parrying, sweeping and hooking with the hand.

The author does not feel any sense of shame for leaving the Shotokan and Wado-Ryu styles, because he, as others have done, has followed the Japanese concept of *SHUHARI*.

The *SHU* - indicates **obedience** to your instructor: the beginner must correctly copy all techniques from his instructor.

The *HA* - indicates **divergence**, after approximately 10-15 years of study you are allowed to create new techniques because you have experienced the effectiveness of those techniques, but the basics and essence must remain the same.

The *RI* - indicates **separation**, it means that now you can separate and your proper technique must follow naturally as your product. This book modestly tries to explain the essence of Sendo-Ryu Karatedo.

The author hopes that this book will be a great help to all Karate instructors and practitioners, because Sendo-Ryu principles can be applied to any Karate style. More importantly, the main Sendo-Ryu principle, which is *Sendo* (the way of initiative), is the essence of life for those who want to succeed.

# I

# INTRODUCTION

Professor Emeric Arus/SOKE - 10th Dan, President and Founder of the International Sendo-Ryu Karatedo Federation and USA Sticky Hands Combat Jujutsu Federation on right, poses in 1996 with his best student/Shihan Dr. Attila Arpad Czegeni 6th Dan, President of the Hungarian Sendo-Ryu Karatedo Federation

# *1.  THE HISTORY OF MARTIAL ARTS*

## Historical background

There is a long history of human combat that is as old as human beings themselves.  At all times and places in the world, human beings must have had to defend themselves against animals with an instinctive fight of survival.  They relied only on their physical strength but later developed fighting techniques and weapons to give an extra chance to survive in a hostile environment.  Fighting methods evolved through the course of centuries, reflecting the needs and specific characteristics of the people and their environments.

As the family evolved as the main social group, awareness of blood ties would have led to the need for defense between clans and groups.  One class of society that arose in that time was the warrior class, where a human being made for himself weapons both for self-defense and for attacking his enemies.

The great civilization of Sumerians, with flourishing arts and philosophy at approximately 3600-3700 years ago, practiced a form of hand-to-hand fighting similar to that of our modern time boxing and wrestling scenes.  Very similar depictions are found on the bas-reliefs of Egyptian tombs that are 3000 years old.

## The beginning of empty hand fighting

### Europe

Before the first Olympic Games (776 BC) there was an event called Pankration.  This was a form of unarmed combat and later it developed into two modern sports of wrestling and boxing.  The Greek civilization furthermore developed and organized wrestling and boxing contests between Athena and Sparta.

### India

The influence of European fighting techniques spread into Asia, first into Persia (331-327 BC), with the invasion of Alexander the Great, and later into India (327-323 BC).  The influence of these fighting methods spread further throughout Asia, especially in India, Mongolia and China, by Buddhist missionaries.  For example, in Thailand, Thaistyle boxing evolved and, in Indonesia, the fighting method was called Pentjak-Silat.

### China

The Indian martial art was introduced into China by a Buddhist monk, named Bodhidharma (Daruma in Japanese), about 1400 years ago. He traveled from a kingdom in Southern India, of which he was the third prince, and settled in the Shaolin Temple (Shorin Ji in Japanese) in the Hao Shan mountains of Hunan province in China. He undertook the teaching of Zen Buddhism, a form of contemplative religion, and also incorporated fighting arts teachings as a necessary way to preserve health. Bodhidharma developed a training method that encompassed the spiritual and physical developments of the Buddhist monks. He asserted that mind, spirit and body are inseparable and have to be treated as a whole. Since the religion that the monks practiced prohibited the use of weapons, they had to rely on these empty hands fighting methods that were known as Shorinji Kenpo.

This physical aspect of Zen Buddhism, so said I-Chin-Ching, was later developed into a complete self-defense method, which become necessary, as the monks were often attacked by highway robbers who were ransacking the country shaken by civil war.

China was shaken by internal dissension between 1840-1901 due to plunder of foreign colonial powers. During this period China had several wars: The Opium war with England in 1840-1842; war against France in 1884; and against Japan in 1894-1895, etc. These wars led to the Boxer Insurrection (the Boxers were an ultra nationalist sect of Kenpo practitioners), crushed by the Ch'ing dynasty in 1901. Many boxers were executed, training houses were closed, and Kenpo was completely eradicated.

This truly Chinese fighting art died and disappeared but, before dying out completely, Kenpo had spread to the Island of Okinawa under the name of Kempo (Japanese version - Kenpo is Chinese version). The Okinawa Island became the place where Karate was born.

## Early development of martial/fighting art

The founder of Zen Buddhism, Bodhidharma, taught his disciples the art of the preservation of health, the eighteen ways of Lo-Han, all of which had a marked influence on Chinese theories of fighting methods. During the so called "Spring-Autumn Period" (770-481 BC), the various arts of fighting, among which was the popular "Chiao Ti Shu" (Kakuteijitsu in Japanese), were highly valued among the noble classes in China.

During the Han period, the Kakuteijitsu fighting method became known as Kaiko. A Chinese named Ch'en Yuan Yun, in 1588, went over to Japan and lived at Shoko-Kuji in Edo (the old name of Tokyo) where he initiated the mysteries of Kakuteijitsu to the Japanese. Tai Chi Ch'uan (Taikyokuken in Japanese) was founded about the time of the end of the Ming dynasty (1644 AD), and the beginning of the Ch'ing dynasty. This fighting art has a history of 280-300 years. The Ch'ing dynasty ended at 1911.

# History of modern Karate in 19th and 20th century

The Shorinji Kempo and a lot of other fighting methods from China, that had spread to the Ryu-Kyu islands, were developed into Okinawa-Te, the forerunner of present day Karate. Okinawan towns, such as Shuri, Naha and Tomari, had major roles in modern Karate development.  Prior to the 15th century, Karate was named just Te (hand), so masters of Shuri taught Shuri-Te, Naha-Te or Tomari-Te.

The most important instructors of Shuri-Te were Sakugawa and Sokon Matsumura, who was called "Shuri Matsumura." Matsumura had a very famous student by the name of Yasutsune Itosu (1830-1915) who introduced Karate into the Okinawan public school curriculum.  Naha town had also two major instructors.  The earlier one was named Arakaki (1840-1920) and his student Kanryo Higaonna (1835-1915).  Higaonna's best student was Chojun Miyagi, the Goju-Ryu style founder.  Tomari-Te were represented by Matsumora (1829-1898) and Oyadomari (1831-1905), but they never reached the popularity of Matsumura, Itosu and Higaonna, but each taught students who later played an important role in the history of Karate.  Karate was also named as Tode in Okinawa.  In August 1905, another Okinawan instructor Nagashige Hanagusuku used the Japanese characters empty hand (Karate) instead of Tode.

In Japan, in about 1930, master Gichin Funakoshi changed Tode to Karate.  At the end of the 19th century Shuri-Te became known as Shorin-Ryu and Naha-Te became known as Shorei-Ryu.  These two styles created the basics of modern Shotokan Karate.  The history of Karate and the literature of specialty consider that the founder of modern era Karatedo is Gichin Funakoshi.  Funakoshi, at the age of 53, went from Okinawa to Japan to propagate Karate.  He studied under the masters Itosu, Yasuzato, Arakaki and Matsumura.

In 1922 Karate was first introduced to the Japanese public.  Funakoshi, who was then a teacher at the Okinawa Teacher's College was invited to lecture and demonstrate an exhibition of traditional martial arts, sponsored by the Ministry of Education.  In 1936, Funakoshi established Shotokan as the great landmark in the history of Karate in Japan.  In the late years of the '50s and the beginning of the '60s, a lot of Karate masters traveled to Europe and America spreading and establishing the art of Karatedo.

# Major Karate schools of the 20th century

The following four styles/schools of Karate are recognized as major styles in Japan:
1. Shito-Ryu, founder Kenwa Mabuni (1893-1957)
2. Goju-Ryu, founder Chojun Miyagi (1888-1953)
3. Shotokan, founder Gichin Funakoshi (1869-1957)
4. Wado-Ryu, founder Hironori Otsuka (1892-1981).  Other Karate schools or systems are:  Jeet Kune Do (Bruce Lee's style);  Hwarang Do (Korean);  Pentjak Silat (Indonesian);  Shorin-Ryu (Okinawan);  Shorinji-Ryu (Japanese);  Uechi-Ryu (Okinawan);  Isshin-Ryu (Okinawan);  Kenyu-Ryu (Japanese);  Kyokushin (Japanese);  Kojo-Ryu (Okinawan) etc.

# 2.   WHAT SENDO-RYU KARATEDO IS

## The philosophy of Sendo-Ryu

Sendo can be translated as "The Way of Initiative." It is well known that in real combat (in the street or in an arena) the person who takes the initiative, whether with attacks, such as Sen No Sen (1) - high initiative, or in defense, such as Go No Sen (2) - initiative in defense has the better chance of winning. Therefore, timing and distances are primary factors in the beginning of the teaching and learning process.

Sendo-Ryu Karatedo uses any part of the body for attacks as well as for defense. It incorporates many takedowns, such as legsweeping, throwing and armlock techniques, from Judo, Jujutsu, Aikijujutsu and Aikido, in order to be victorious in any realistic combat situation. Basically, Sendo-Ryu is a style of speed that focuses on the use of timing and distance between the opponents. The methodology of teaching the sparring is very different from other styles.

The Kata in Sendo-Ryu are very realistic and almost never repeat the same blocks without a counter and seldom use attacks or blocks in the same line repeatedly. Body shifts and evasions are largely used in the blocks as well as in attacks of this style.

Sendo-Ryu Karatedo philosophy is a hard concept about living every day and doing things by working as hard as possible to make it easier later on. It never stops seeking the culmination of character, cultivation of old traditions of Budo -- honesty, loyalty, and humbleness -- but receptive to everything that is new and useful in order to make things better and analyzing yourself with maximum exigency at all times.

The teaching philosophy of Sendo-Ryu has no secret method-techniques. The founder's method of teaching is a simple one:  Teach and practice every day to help you find new ways of efficiency in your style.

Sendo-Ryu philosophy about fighting is simple:  In fighting, there are no positions; the fighter anticipates any attack from his opponent and the counter is never delayed.

# 3.  *THE UNDERSTANDING AND PRACTICE OF KARATE*

## The Kihon, Kata, Kumite and Tameshiwari

General Karate training has three inseparable parts:  Basic practice (Kihon), formal exercises (Kata) and sparring (Kumite).  It also has other additional and very important training parts, such as punching board (Makiwara) practice; breaking practice (Tameshiwari); and special stretching, conditioning training with many diversified equipments.  All these parts are aspects used to develop physical qualities, such as speed, strength, endurance, skill and ability to convert all these aspects to develop psychological, mental and moral qualities.

### Basic practice (Kihon)

Kihon is the main tool for self-discipline and the muscular engine or mechanism of Karate.  The basic practice within a group creates a better atmosphere for self-discipline, but the practice also can be individual.  For beginners, this part of Karate is the most important.  Practice of combination techniques is also a part of Kihon.  This is where techniques, balances and body coordinations are developed.

### Formal exercises (Kata)

Kata is considered by almost all Karate experts as the "Soul of Karate."  Kata develops self-discipline and self-confidence in the Karateka, because it contains all physical and mental aspects found in Karate, such as balance, rhythm, speed, strength, endurance, bodyshifting, breathing, fighting spirit by using the shout (Kiai) and perfect mental alertness (Zanshin).  Kata is the main tool in Karate for technical improvements.  Experts said that all the form (Kata) in a certain style practiced and understood correctly is the "Art of Karatedo."

### Sparring - fighting (Kumite)

Kumite is the essence of Karate, especially free fighting (Jiyu Kumite).  Karate has also pre and established sparring.  The 1 - 2 - 3 steps or preestablished fighting methods, like Kihon Kata Kumite are very important.  They also merge into Jiyu Kumite.  When people enter for the first time in a Karate gym (Dojo), they would like to learn a very effective self-defense method to protect themselves by fighting well.  Later on they discover that Karate is not only a self-defense method, but also an excellent physical education method.

It is well known that Karate is a scientific fighting method.  In the early development of Karate, free fighting did not exist, because the masters were afraid of many injuries that happened much earlier in time.  That is why the way of teaching Karate was only by the practice of Kata.  The best fighting spirit and the experience of fighting can be obtained only by Kumite, especially by Jiyu Kumite.  In Jiyu Kumite you are faced with a real opponent and you have to use all your physical and mental energies to be victorious.

Another factor of Jiyu Kumite is the sport competition (Shiai).  Karate sport competitions are important especially for the youths.  Competitions give more motivation for a harder training.  Competitions can also be bad for Karate.  Many times the purpose excuses the means that the Karateka does regrettable actions in order to be victorious  (uncontrolled and prohibited executions) which may be the cause of many accidents.

Jiyu Kumite helps develop good character, because the Karateka learns to control his fist, by stopping one inch from the opponent's face.  You do not want to win, in any way, as in a sport competition.  Jiyu Kumite is a free style, soft controlled fight.  In Jiyu Kumite the Karateka must be first winner against himself and the Karateka should dominate his aggressiveness, by using well-focused techniques with a great muscular control, namely to stop hitting or kicking his opponent.

In a non-contact Karate system, if you are able not to touch your opponent, that is to say, you can control your emotions, then your opponent becomes your partner.  This does not mean that your aggressiveness suffers, because you are not hitting someone well.  You can develop your aggressiveness in many ways, for example, by contact of full contact Karate, by practicing breaking techniques on woods, bricks, ices etc.  Focusing your attack and energy by stopping just in front of your opponent is a sublimation of your energy and impulses.

The sublimation of your impulses affects positively your mental attitude to become a better human being, however, one must first know and search his human character.  Every fight is a new challenge to discover and know better your attitude and character and also your partner's character, temperament and thinking.

If your partner is very dangerous, then you have to excel in other ways than fighting with him brutally.  In this state of mind you should fight rather strategically.  When your life is in danger, you should act using adequate attacks or ripostes, according to how dangerous your opponent's attacks are.  Jiyu Kumite gives you the best self-confidence.  Who is the loser, or who is the winner, is not the main objective of Karate.  The ultimate objective of Karatedo is the cultivation of your character through rigorous training.

**Breaking practice (Tameshiwari)**

Tameshiwari is a method used in Karate for testing your courage, speed, power, precision, technique, concentration, aggressiveness and even skill.  In order to be a successful breaker, you must train hard on punching board (Makiwara) and punching bag (Sutanawara). Tameshiwari helps greatly in the development of one's self-confidence.

Practicing correctly and constantly Kihon, Kata, Kumite will develop one's own method of self-defense.

# 4.   *THE THEORY OF KARATE*

## Biomechanical, physiological and psychological principles

**Center of gravity** - (Fig. 1)  The stomach (Hara) is the spiritual center of the human body, according to Japanese experts.  The center of gravity (C.G.) is defined in biomechanics as the imaginary point (approximate 3-4 cm under the navel), representing the weight center of an object, where all parts exactly balance each other.  The C.G. is closely related with body stability and balance.  Any technique executed in any direction must keep the C.G. at constant correct level.  This means that the Hara must be kept rose upwards, in this way the balance can be maintained.  Any loss of balance creates a bad technique with less power and this means the loss of efficiency in attack or defense (weak penetration power in attack or weak defense in blocking.)

**Body rotation power** - (Fig. 2)  A great majority of dynamic force utilized in Karate techniques are all generated by rotating the body and more importantly, by rotating the hips. Hips' rotation is essential in the need for stronger Karate techniques, both in defense and in offense.  With hip rotation the power from the trunk and abdomen muscles travel to the spine which in turn acts as a stabilizing mechanism and shock absorber.  The power continues on to the chest and arm muscles, to the punching fist.

Fig. 1

Body rotation:  Relation between withdrawing hand and hip rotation.

Fig. 2

In kicking techniques the shock absorber is the supporting leg.  Beginners cannot get proper hip power rotation and that is why their techniques are less effective.  Any Karate technique's execution starts with rotating the hips, these being the slowest and the heaviest parts of the body.  Reaction force is also applied to Karate techniques by body and hip rotation, by pressing hard against the floor with the rear leg in case of punching or striking.

**Focus (Kime)** (Photo A)  The concentration and eliberation of maximum power in the shortest time possible is the Kime.  This factor is the key to technical effectiveness.  During any technical execution, the working muscles, as well as other body muscles, must be kept in a relaxed position; only at the final impact must the muscles be tensed then immediately relaxed again.  Muscles, tendons and body postures must be kept in a relaxed position at all times to allow reflex responses to changing situations.

**Rhythm (Ri Ai)**   This is especially important in Kata in order to perform succesfully the slow or fast techniques which change with rhythm.  In fighting situation when you execute combination techniques the rhythm is an essential factor.

Focus (Kime) - Photo A - Demonstration of glass breaking safely:
5 glasses superposed.

**Breathing** - Execution of techniques with correct rhythm helps maintain proper breathing.  Improper breathing brings about the absence of power and loss of endurance in fighting.  Correct breathing involves an inhale at the beginning of any execution, which can be short or long in time, and an exhale at the end of execution that is always short in Jiyu Kumite and sometimes long in Kata execution.  In a long exhale situation the execution is longer in time and the muscles (abdominal and executor muscles of the arm or leg) are tensed at all times.  This kind of long exhale does not exist in fighting, but only in Kata executions.

### Distance - (Ma) - (Fig. 3),  Timing, Speed (Hayasa)

These three factors are vital to free fighting.  In free fighting, in order to be efficient, you must first adjust the distance, then the timing.  When the distance is too short between you and your opponent, then you are in the opponent's range and he may attack you first.  When the distance is too long, then there is a good chance you could telegraph your attack and this could be intercepted with a strong stopping attack, a strong block or simply your opponent will avoid by shifting his body.

Even if the distance is correct for an attack, but you start late, this means your timing is incorrect.

The speed is closely related to the distance.  From the shortest distance (Chika Ma), when your arm is an extended position, it can reach your opponent - close range, your attack will have good speed, but less power.  From medium range (Uchi Ma) distance, your attack will have the maximum efficiency, you will obtain the maximum speed, maximum power and the best balance.  From long range distance (To Ma), you can lose the speed along with the power and the balance as well.  Speed is also a key element, not only in Karate, but in any other sport as well.

### Shout - (Kiai)

This is the materialization of internal power which is the Ki.  This shout is the shortest explosion in time from the Hara, which is usually expelled at the finalization of the attack or defense even in a throwing action.  The Kiai assumes a short term physical action.  When the Kiai occurs, then the technique is executed with focus (Kime).  The sound is similar to: Ki Ai, Ei Ai,  Ei Ia,  Ki Ha,  Ki Aai etc.  The sound comes out from lower abdomen (Hara or Tanden), not from the thoracic region, and not from the throat.  From the lower abdominal region the residue air is liberated, by strong pressure to the upper part of the diaphragm.

Short range distance
(Chika Ma)

Medium range distance
(Uchi Ma)

Long range distance
(To Ma)

Distance (Ma) - Fig. 3

**Meditation (Mokuso) - (Fig. 4)**

Meditation is as important for the mind as physical exercises are for the body. Meditation is a reflection on oneself in order to perceive oneself. Usually Karate training starts and ends with meditation. People should make a difference between meditation and concentration. In concentrating, the mind is fixed on one single subject or thought and excludes all other thoughts.

Meditation is a tool for deep relaxation, when the electrical waves generated by the brain slow down approximately 50 %. This is the state of restful awareness, which is named the Alpha level, and emanates 7-14 energy impulses per second. The total awareness, or consciousness state of the mind, is named the Beta level and the energy impulses are between 14-21 per second.

While the physical process is an active act, meditation is the psychological act that transcends the usual limitations of human consciousness and expands to higher limits of awareness. By correct meditation you can develop a strong mental attitude by emptying the mind of any thought and, by this process, bringing you peace and calmness of mind allowing it to harmonize itself with the universe.

The stillness realized during meditation also slows down the body's metabolism. This provides a deep state of rest which has great therapeutic benefits by rejuvenating the entire body, especially the nervous system and the cardiovascular system. Whatever effort you do put into meditation, it comes back to you many times over, so that your life begins to prolongate in ways you had never imagined. However, some meditations concentrate on breathing, while others on a sound or by focusing the mind on the circulation of the internal energy (Ki).

The best meditation position is the Padmasana - Lotus (Yoga), or Seiza, or Agura position (legs are crossed in front of your body), you have to put under your bottom a small pillow, which helps your abdomen position to be pushed forward, essential in breathing; straighten your back and put your shoulders down, pushing your stomach forward with correct centripetal pressure; put your hands on your thighs in a completely relaxed position with your fingers lightly closed; keep your eyes and mouth closed, but without any pressure; inhale from the nose and fully lift your diaphragm at each inhalation, while tensing slightly your abdominal muscles; exhale from a slightly open mouth. The concentration on breathing is the key in avoiding mind disturbances.

Meditation positions

Seiza or Zazen

Agura

Fig. 4

# II

## THE TRAINING AND METHODOLOGY

# 1.  KARATE TRAINING LESSON

## Warm-up (Taiso)

Any training session (sport lesson) of Karate or other sport has three different and major parts, which are unified as a whole.

**These three parts are:**

*1.  Warm-up 15-20 minutes.*
*2.  Basic training part* -- Karate technical skill, conditioning 65-70 minutes.
*3. Cool-down,* including supplementary and stretching exercises 3-7 minutes, sometimes 10 minutes.  These time sets are for 1 hour and 30 minutes lessons.  Warm-up can be done in many different ways depending on the objective of basic training.

It is well known that an inactive human body which is sitting, standing, or just walking needs less energy than a body in a full fitness activity like Karate.  If you try rope jumping, at the beginning you feel a sensation of heaviness but, with time, rope skipping becomes easier and smoother to perform.

**Warming-up exercises have the:**

*Physical objectives* -- Skeletal -- muscular preparation for effort
                     -- Physiological preparation for effort

*Psychological objectives* -- Relaxation of body and mind, also mental alertness

Warm-up elevates your blood pressure and heart beat, which help consequently for a better blood circulation, bringing more oxygen to the tissues and opening more blood vessels for the elevated effort.  Body temperature rises with the air ventilation.  The body temperature will rise up from 36.6 Celsius to 37.4 Celsius degrees in 12-15 minutes of work.  Pulmonary ventilation can elevate 10-15 times more during effort.  Such respiratory volume in a resting position is 8 liter/minute, and at the end of warm-up it can reach up to 40-55 liter/minute, even more.  Usually, in warm-up, we use three categories of exercises:

*a) Jumping, jogging, running* (light athletics -- track and field exercises).

*b) Calisthenics* (including floor gymnastics exercises).

*c) Flexibility* -- stretching exercises.

Warm-up exercises can be done as isotonic (dynamic), isometric (static) and intermediate isometric.  Jumping and running exercises, as well as for neck, arms, shoulders, hips, knees, or feet rotations, inclinations and twisting should be done dynamically.

Flexibility -- stretching exercises can be done dynamically as well as statically.  The dynamic stretching is also named ballistic stretching which is the oldest method of stretching that uses repetitive bouncing motions.  Static exercises means contracting the muscles against any object, such as floor, chair or arm against arm etc.,  or contracting the muscles without any movement.

Flexibility has been defined as the ability to move a joint or series of joints through a full, nonrestricted, pain-free range of motion.  For stretching the static exercises are recommended, because there is less possibility to incur muscle strain.  The static stretching is also named as passive range of motion (3).  In static stretching no muscle contraction is involved, a joint may be passively moved (by the athlete itself or by somebody else) to the endpoints (4) in the range of motion.  Intermediate isometric exercises means contracting the muscles to the maximum and doing some motion very slowly, such as, push-ups, squat-ups etc.

Because Karate is a very dynamic sport is the reason why dynamic exercises are more highly recommended than others.  Also, if isometric exercises are done with 100 % of muscle contraction against obstacles -- objects, they must be done carefully, because the contraction is done anaerobically (5) which can cause dizziness and later brain damage.  The isometric exercises are done for between 6-12 seconds.

The following pages contain a general warm-up program methodically described and shown later on by photos, see (Photos 1 to 49).

*A.  Running:*

1.   With the knee raised up high -- approx. 20-30 seconds (Photo 1).
2.   Sideways crossing of the legs -- 15 seconds (Photo 2).
3.   Backwards and many different ways etc.

*B.  Jumping:*

1.   Leaping -- legs are bent -- approx. 20 seconds (Photo 3).
2.   Squat jumping with advancement -- 3 x 8 (12) yards.
3.   Leaping -- legs are extended frontally into air -- approx. 4-5 times (Photo 4).
4.   Leaping -- legs are extended laterally into air and simultaneously with both legs or crossing the legs -- approx. 10 times.
5.   Jumping forwards and backwards -- 10 times.

6. From lunge position, jumping up and landing down into a lunge position, changing the legs over in the air -- approx. 6 + 6 times (Photo 5).

C. *Softening* -- limbering the body:

1. Neck rotation (circumduction), flexion, extension, inclination laterally -- approx. 10 + 10 times (Photo 6).
2. Rotate the arms -- warming up the shoulders -- 10 times forward, 10 times backward (Photos 7, 8).
3. Lifting up one arm and let down the other -- approx. 10 times (Photo 9).
4. Lifting together both arms laterally up and down -- approx. 8 - 10 times (Photo 10).
5. Rotate the hips, palms are on the kidneys -- approx. 5 + 5 times (Photo 11).
6. Twist your body -- approx. 2 x 8 repetitions.
7. Bend your body -- to the front -- to the side and backwards, straighten up -- approx. 4 + 4 + 4 times (Photos 12, 13).
8. Rotate your upper body, arms kept together -- approx. 3 + 3 rest few seconds, then 3 + 3 times again (Photo 13).
9. Raise your knee to the chest (alternate your legs) 10 + 10 times (Photo 14).
10. Take Shiko Dachi position, lowering and elevating your weight approx. 5-6 times (Photos 15, 16).
11. Rotate the knees -- palms are on the knees -- approx. 5 + 5 times (Photo 17).
12. Bend your toes and sit on them and come back on a standing position approx. 5 times (Photos 18, 19).
13. From a slightly lunge position swing one leg forward as high as possible -- approx. 10 + 10 times (Photo 20).
14. Push-ups on palms, on fists, on edge of the palms, on fingers or one arm etc. (Photos 21, 22).
15. From standing position bend your body forward and down, the fingers touching the toes (legs are together), hold this position for a few seconds (Photo 23).
16. Very wide standing position (legs are kept very wide apart) touch the floor with your elbows and move on your forearms forward to extend your hips (Photos 24, 25).
17. Sitting position, left leg in front, right leg above left, turn your torso to the right -- keep the position -- 10 seconds (Photo 26), then change the legs position -- 10 seconds.
18. Warm-up the ankles and toes rotating them (Photo 27).
19. Sit on Seiza, warm-up your fingers and wrists twisting them easily (Photos 28, 29).
20. Sitting position, grab your toes and pull your feet, aiming heels at your groin, whilst bending your body forward (Photos 30, 31).

*D.  Exercises for abdomen:*

1.  Lie on your back, arms are extended  behind your head.  Sit up and pull your knees to your chin grasping them with your forearms, then lie down and repeat -- 15 times (Photos 32, 33, 34).
2.  Lie on your back, arms are extended behind your head.  Execute Jack-Knife position, then lie down and repeat -- 15 times (Photos 35, 36).
3.  Abdomen exercises with partner.

*E.  Other exercises:*

1.  For back muscles -- Waving on the abdomen (rolling back and forth) -- (Photo 37).
2.  From Zenkutsu Dachi position, lift one leg to the shoulder (the rear leg) and let down -- 10 times, then change the position and lift the other leg -- 10 times.
3.  Hold a chair, or a partner, and lift one of your leg sideways -- 10 times (Photo 38).
4.  Sit down with legs apart.  Move in front on your fist, stay, then rest on your forearms, stretch while you are in a side split position, hold approx. 10 - 15 seconds (Photos 39, 40, 41).
5.  Sit down with legs apart.  Twist your upper body, stretch your thigh muscles -- hold approx. 10 - 15 seconds (Photo 42).
6.  From a side lunge position, alternate bending your left and right knee.  Soften the knee joints and groin (Photos 43, 44).
7.  Stretch your legs with a partner, your back against the wall, with one leg lifted over his shoulder in a side kick or a front kick position (both Karateka are in standing position)
8.  Breathing exercises 4 - 6 times (Photos 45, 46, 47, 48).

*A. Running*

*B. Jumping*

Photo 1

Photo 2

Photo 3

*B. Jumping*

Photo 4

Photo 5

*C. Softening - limbering the body*

Photo 6

Photo 7

Photo 8

Photo 9

Photo 10

Photo 11

Photo 12

Photo 13

Photo 14

Photo 15

Photo 16

Photo 17

Photo 18          Photo 19          Photo 20

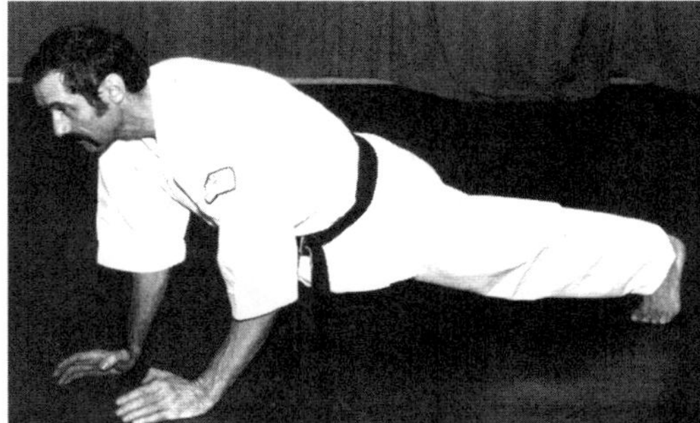

Photo 21

Photo 22

Photo 23

Photo 24

Photo 25

Photo 26

Photo 27

Photo 28

Photo 29

Photo 30

Photo 31

## D. *Exercises for abdomen*

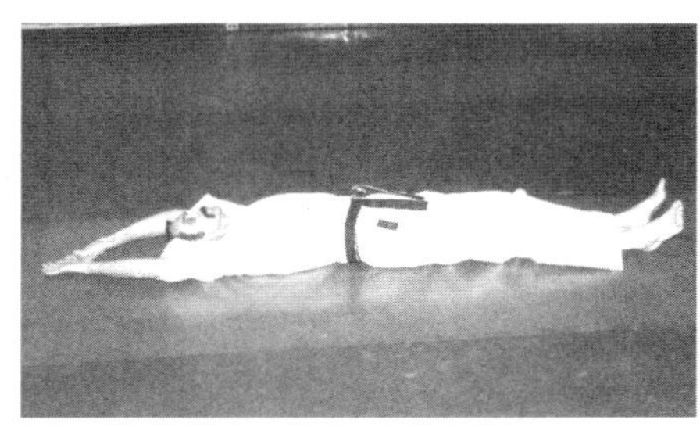

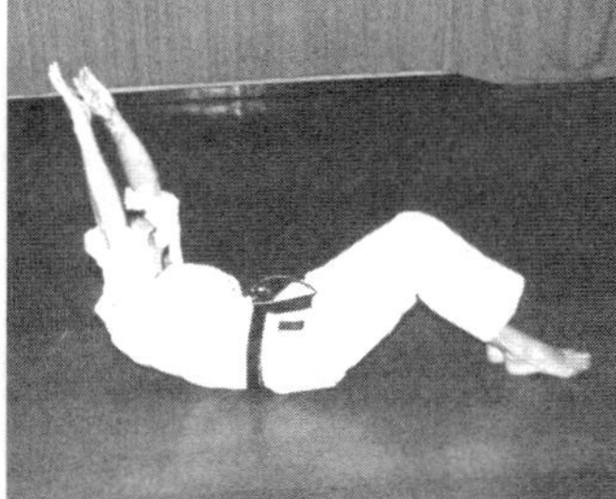

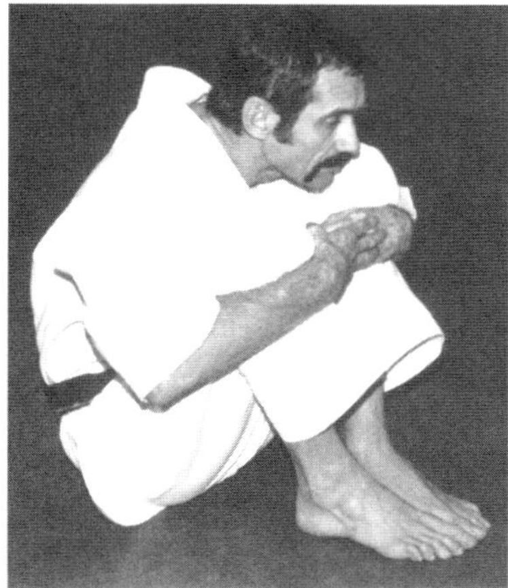

Photo 32

Photo 33

Photo 34

## E. *Other exercises*

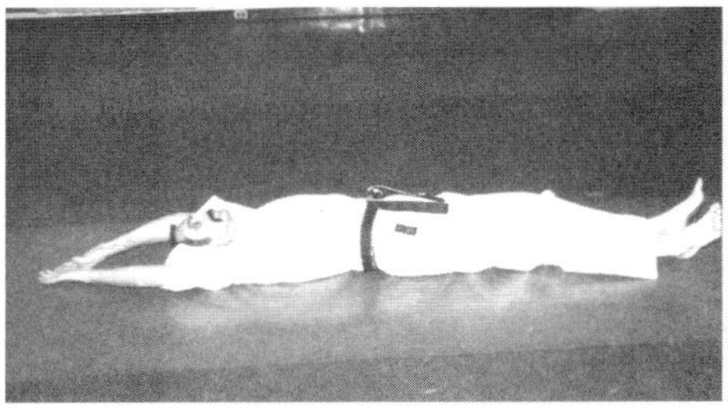

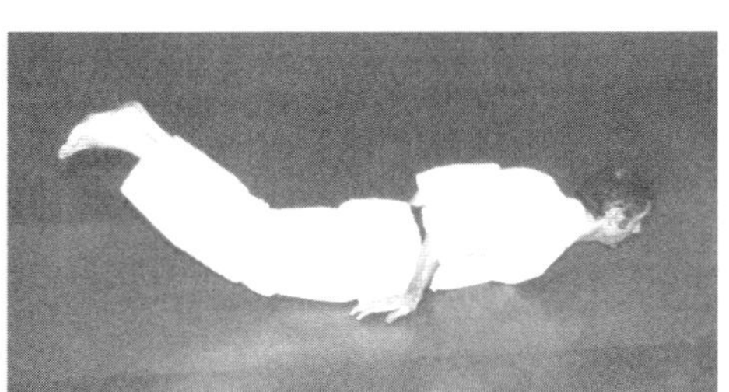

Photo 35

Photo 36

Photo 37

Photo 39

Photo 40

Photo 38

Photo 41

Photo 42

Photo 43

Photo 44

IBUKI breathing method featuring a long exhalation, followed by a short cough to expel the last of the air

Exhale loudly while strengthening your abdomen muscles

Photo 45

Photo 46

NOGARE soft breathing method

Photo 47

Photo 48

Inhale smoothly while expanding your stomach first then your chest

# 2. THE BASICS (Kihon)

## Objectives, principles, classifications

In basic training the student learns the most simple and basic body coordination principles dealing with body mechanics, center of gravity, coordination of body movements, contraction and decontraction of muscles, speed acceleration and deceleration etc.

The basic training purpose is to learn the most economical way of training with the most economical Karate techniques and preparing the body for future hard confrontations which can happen later on in Karate sparring. Also, another purpose of basic training is to create the best basics for reflex mechanism by many repetitions, which is a successful tool for a better technique.

At the beginning of Karate trainings, the most basic stances and postures are taught because in every execution of a punch, kick or block the Karateka must have a good balanced stable position. Also, different positions are used for different techniques.

# 2.1. STANCES (Tachi Kata), POSTURES (Kamae)

The stances of Karate deal mainly with the positioning of the legs, providing the upper body with a strong and stable base needed to supply both strength and ease of motion.

## Stances are classified as follows:
(See Figs. 5 to 22 and Photos 1 to 15)

**1 - Natural stances (Shizentai)**
**2 - Unequal stances or basic stances (Kihon Dachi) - Balanced**
**3 - Equal stances or basic stances (Kihon Dachi) - Balanced**
**4 - Other (Varied) stances - Unbalanced**
**5 - Fighting stances (Kumite Dachi)**

# 1 - Natural stances (Shizentai)

**Feet - Together Stances:**

**a** - Feet-Together Stance (Heisoku Dachi) (Fig. 5 & Photo 1)

The feet are placed side by side, the entire body is postured at a vertical angle with the arms held slightly apart from the body, together in front of the body, or at the side of the body. This position is slightly balanced, used usually for Kata.  Serious Karate actions are limited from this position.

**b** - Informal Attention Stance (Musubi Dachi) (Fig. 6 & Photo 2)

The heels are placed together and the toes are pointed outward, the arms are placed in the same position as in Heisoku Dachi, but this position is better balanced in every direction than Heisoku Dachi.  Musubi Dachi can be better used as a fighting position than Heisoku Dachi.

**Open - Leg Stances:**

**a** - Open-Leg Stance (Hachiji Dachi or Shizentai) (Fig. 7 & Photo 3)

This position is the most relaxed of the natural stances and most suitable for any Karate action.  The position is used as a starting and finishing position in Kata in almost any Japanese Karate style.  The awareness is more intensified in this position than in other natural stances. The feet are placed apart about the width of the hips and the toes pointed outwards at a 25 degrees angle.  The stability is good for more executions of Karate techniques.  This is a basic position for beginners to execute punching, striking, blocking and kicking.

**b** - Parallel Stance (Heiko Dachi) (Fig. 8 & Photo 4)

This position is one of the most important in Sendo-Ryu Karatedo among the natural stances.  The feet are apart about the width of the hips and are parallel to each other.  This position has a good balance.  The feet are held parallel, the knees are pointed inward.  This is why the muscle tension is greater, especially in the lower legs, where tension is transmitted upwards to the brain giving more awareness, even if this position is a natural relaxed position.

The execution of the different techniques are easily made from this position.

**c** - Inverted Open-Leg Stance (Uchi Hachiji Dachi) (Fig. 9)

This is the most stable stance among the natural stances, but it is rarely used because of the uncomfortable position of the feet and knees.  It is used by the most skillful and advanced Karateka.

**Right Angle Stances:**

**a** - Natural Stance, left or right (Hidari or Migi Shizentai) or (Renoji Dachi) (Fig. 10)

If the left leg is in front, it is called Hidari Shizentai.  This position is used often by Aikido, Kendo and high ranked Karate masters.  The legs are completely extended, but relaxed all over.  The mobility is very good and this stance is used as a turning point for many body shifting - turning (Tai Sabaki).

**b** - "T" Stance (Teiji Dachi) (Fig. 11)

This position is less stable than the stance described before and is balanced toward the back foot.  It is used also by Aikido and Kendo practicioners.

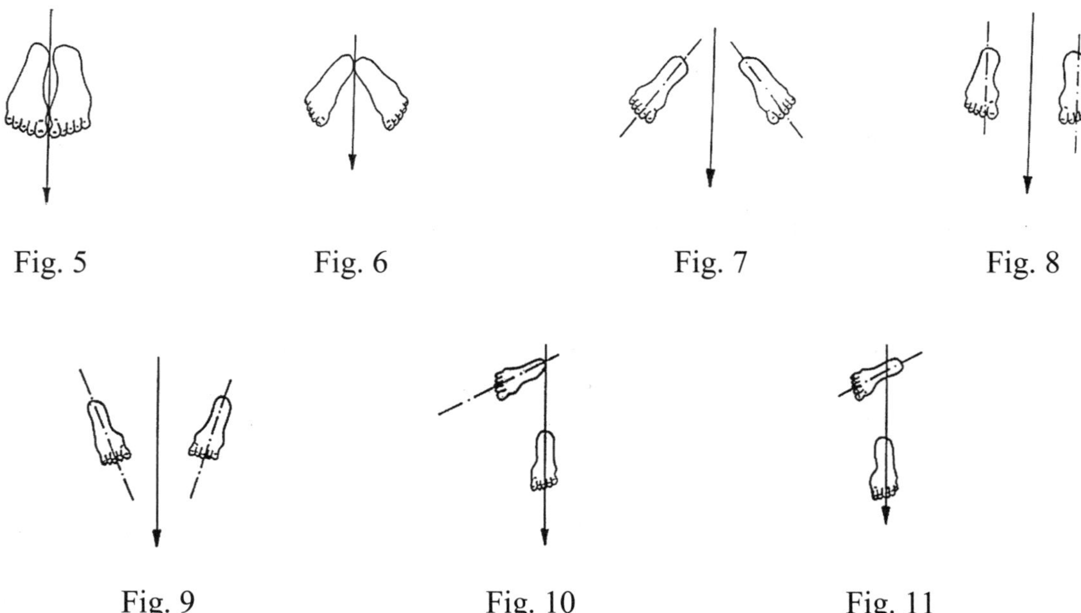

Fig. 5          Fig. 6          Fig. 7          Fig. 8

Fig. 9          Fig. 10          Fig. 11

Photo 1          Photo 2          Photo 3          Photo 4

## 2 - Unequal stances or basic stances (Kihon Dachi)

Basic or fundamental stances are characterized by the factors of stability, strength and technical accuracy.  Every basic stance can be held in a high or low position.  The most difficult thing is to find the optimal position which should be neither too high nor too low.  However, it is well known that the lower the position the stabler and stronger it becomes, but loses its mobility of change.

We know certainly that for any execution of a Karate technique the stance must ensure a high degree of speed, strength and ability for repetition (endurance) and, of course, technical skill.  The recommended optimal position for beginners is to use the very low position, especially during the repetition of basic techniques.  Later on, when the student has improved its technical skills, then the positions can be higher.  The low position builds up stronger muscles in the legs which give confidence for stable positions.

For speed, technical skill and endurance, the very low stance is not recommended.  Low stances reduce the mobility of technical executions and that of the changing positions.  A decrease in endurance also does not permit the use of a low position for a long time.  The correct advice for the optimal position should be as follows:

The very low positions should be used when the student is working on body conditioning for strength and endurance.  When the student is working for speed or skill, the positions must be kept higher.  In tournaments, where the body weight is kept most of the time in a low position, the Karateka becomes tired, because the thigh muscles (especially the quadriceps muscles) are tightened.  In this way body shifts are also made difficult as a result of tiredness.

**a** - Front Stance (Zenkutsu Dachi) (Fig. 12 & Photo 5)

The front knee is bent and the rear leg is extended with the knee slightly bent. The front knee vertical line projection to the ground meets the second phalanges of the foot. This position is mainly used for attack, but can be used for defense too. Weight is supported as follows: Front leg 60-70 %, rear leg 30-40 %. The feet are apart from each other at shoulder distance. This position is relatively strong for both front and rear, (Fig. 12) shows the feet projection when Jun Zuki is performed. When the reverse punch (Gyaku Zuki) is performed, the feet are projected at a wider distance than the shoulders, and the distance between the legs in front and back is shorter. The variation of Zenkutsu Dachi is Half Front Stance (Han Zenkutsu Dachi), where the front leg and the rear leg are closer to each other.

**b** - Back Stance (Kokutsu Dachi) (Fig. 13 & Photo 6)

This stance is mainly used for defense and it can frequently be seen in Kata and the least in free fighting, as it is pretty difficult to master this position. In the case of right back stance (Migi Kokutsu Dachi) the right leg is back and supporting 60 % of the body weight; meanwhile the left leg is in front and is supporting 40 % of the body weight.
The stability is not as great as Zenkutsu Dachi, but it is stable enough backwards. The heels are in the same line, with the feet making a 90 degrees angle projection between them. The center of gravity is closer to the rear foot. Therefore, holding this position for a long time could be very difficult, especially for the rear leg.
Tiredness and pain is to be expected, especially in the knee cap and the thigh of the back leg. This position must be alternated all the time with other positions to ease the tiredness.

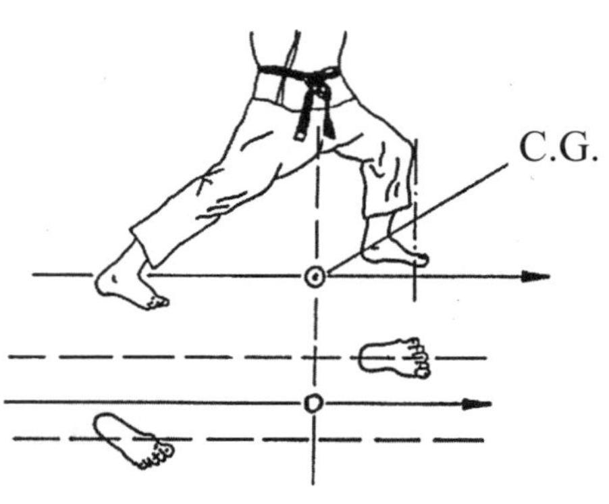


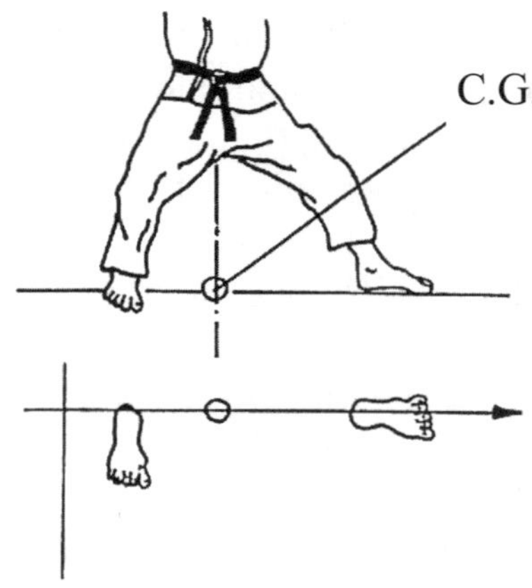


Fig. 12                                        Fig. 13

Photo 5

Photo 6

# 3 - Equal stances or basic stances (Kihon Dachi)

Classified here are the stances in which the weight is supported by both legs equally, or almost equally.

**a -** Straddle-Leg Stance (Kiba Dachi) (Fig. 14 & Photo 7)

This stance is also known as Horse Stance or Knight Stance, because the legs are bent in such a way reminiscent of a horse riding position.  The feet are apart at the distance of 1 and 1/2 distance of the shoulders.  Feet are parallel, strongly planted into the ground.  The external edges of the feet must be parallel and not the inside edges.  The center of gravity is exactly halfway between the feet.  The knees are pressed outward.  This position is very stable to the sides and is less stable to the front and even less stable to the back.

If the distance between the feet is larger than 1 1/2 shoulder width, then the stance is stronger, more stable and less mobile  When the distance is smaller than 1 1/2 shoulder width, the stance is less stable, but has more mobility.

The upper body must always be kept straight and erect vertically.  The leg muscles must be tensed all the time.  The feet are planted with the toes pressed firmly to the ground.  The hips and the navel must be kept in upright position.  This also helps for better breathing.  Kiba Dachi is used well in Kata and also in Kumite.

**b -** Squat Stance (Shiko Dachi) (Fig. 15 & Photo 8)

This stance is also known as Sumo Dachi because the legs are bent like the Sumo wrestlers at the beginning of matches as a ritual exercise for leg relaxation and fortification of the hips.  This position is deeper than the Straddle-Leg Stance.  The feet are kept on the same line laterally and the toes are directed outward about 45 degrees angle.  Holding this position for a longer time than other positions is pretty difficult because the quadriceps muscles are extremely well used.  To perform this position in a very deep manner, a long time of practice is required.  The knees are usually bent at 45 degrees angle and the thighs tend to be parallel with the ground.

**c - Half-Moon Stance (Hangetsu Dachi) (Fig. 16 & Photo 9)**

This stance has a great stability in any direction and, at the same time, gives the fighter a very confident feeling.  The center of gravity is exactly between the two legs with the knees tensed inward.  This position is suitable for defense, as well as for attack, but mainly for defense.  Because the knees are oriented inward, the position gives some protection against a groin attack.  Stability is very good.  The distance between the feet is approximately two shoulder widths.  For best stability, the legs and the lower abdominal muscles must be contracted.

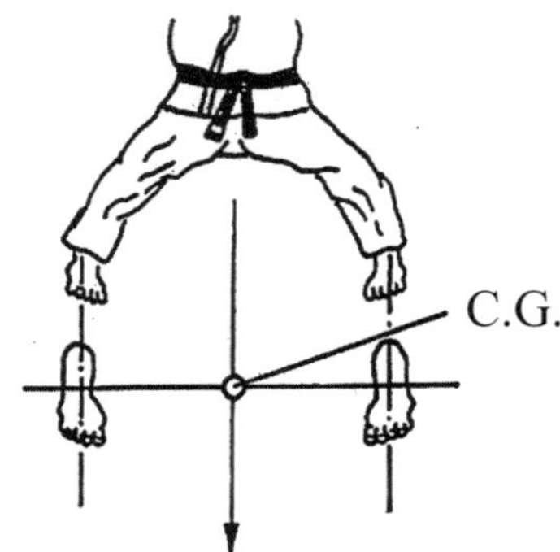


Fig. 14

Fig. 16

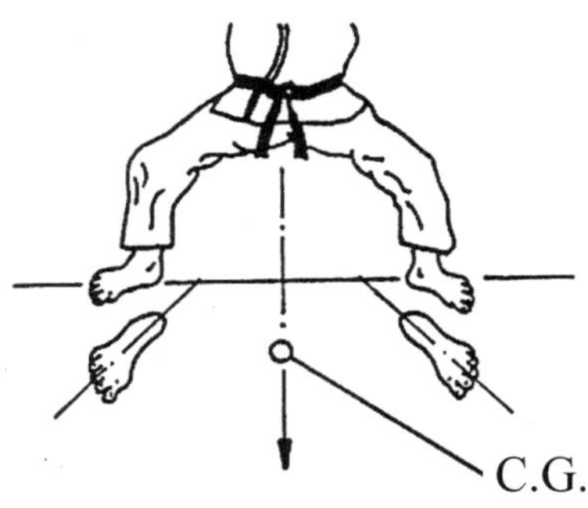


Fig. 15

Photo 7

Photo 8

Photo 9

**d -** Rooted Stance (Fudo Dachi) (Fig. 17 & Photo 10)

It is also known as Sochin Dachi, which is used especially in the Sochin Kata. The Fudo Dachi stance is similar to Kiba Dachi. As in Kiba Dachi, the center of gravity is exactly between the two feet and the distance is exactly the same as in Kiba Dachi.

The two feet are parallel, but faced both 45 degrees angle to the left or to the right depending on the position. For example, in the left rooted stance, the left foot is in front and both feet are faced 45 degrees angle to the right. Both knees are bent and tensed outward. The front knee is bent and tensed forward a little more than the rear knee. The torso must be kept straight forward or twisted a little to the right in the case of the left rooted stance. Mobility is pretty good. This is a very good position especially for defense. This position develops good leg muscles.

**e -** Hourglass Stance (Sanchin Dachi) (Fig. 18 & Photo 11)

This is relatively a high position with knees slightly bent inward. The front foot is turned inward approximately 30 degrees angle. The front foot heel is in the same line with the rear foot toes. The weight of the body is equally supported by both legs. The buttocks are tensed strongly. This position is not very mobile, but the stability is pretty good. This position can be used for attacks, as well as for defense, but it is more widely used for defense. The groin protection is very good because the feet are closer than in Hangetsu Dachi which looks like Sanchin Dachi. The Hangetsu Dachi stance is wider than the Sanchin Dachi stance.

**f -** Fighting Stance (Mae Seishan Dachi or Tate Seishan Dachi) (Fig. 19 & Photo 12)

This position is the most important in the Sendo-Ryu Karate style.  The reason is that this position is strong enough to be used very well for defense, but it is very relaxed and elastic, which is also good for attack situations.  The body is in a relaxed position with the knees slightly bent and oriented straight toward the toes.  The center of gravity is exactly between the two feet.

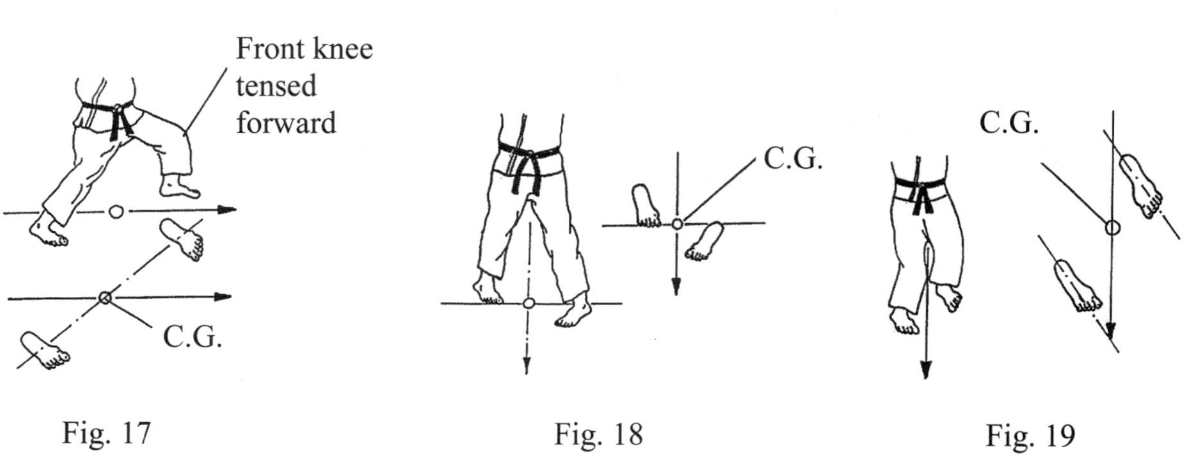


Fig. 17          Fig. 18          Fig. 19

Photo 10          Photo 11          Photo 12

# 4 - Other (varied) stances

**a** - Cat-Leg Stance (Neko Ashi Dachi) (Fig. 20 & Photo 13)

This is an unbalanced stance.  The back leg supports 90-95 percent of the body's weight.  The center of gravity is close to the rear leg heel.  The rear foot's sole is completely down and the toe is positioned at the angle in excess of 45 degrees.  The front leg ball of the foot has contact with the ground.  Both knees are bent approximately 130-150 degrees angle, but the front knee is kept just slightly bent.  This stance has a pretty good flexibility and the ability to execute attacks with the front leg.  Holding this position is pretty difficult because the rear - supporting leg (quadriceps muscle) becomes tired.

**b** - Cross-Leg Stance (Kosa Dachi) (Fig. 21 & Photo 14)

This stance is more unbalanced than the Cat-Leg Stance.  Here the rear leg somehow becomes pushed forward and almost becomes a front leg supporting position.  The front leg supports approximately 90 percent of the body's weight, this supporting leg's sole is firmly pressing the ground.  The supporting leg's knee is oriented forward.  Both knees are bent sufficiently for an approximate 100-110 degrees angle, but the rear is somehow less bent and has a greater mobility to change into other stances.  By bending the supporting leg's knee more, this will increase the stability, but decrease the mobility.  In the right Cross-Leg Stance position, the left leg passes behind the right leg, so the left toes point at the edge of the right foot and the ball of the foot has the contact with the ground.  This stance can be seen mainly in Kata.

**c** - One-Leg Stance (Sagi Ashi Dachi or Tsuru Ashi Dachi) (Fig. 22 & Photo 15)

In this stance the body weight is practically on one leg.  The raised foot (instep) placed behind the knee or the sole can be placed to the inside of the supporting leg's knee.  The raised leg is often used for different kicks, especially side kicks.  Like the Cross-Leg Stance, it can be seen mainly in Kata.

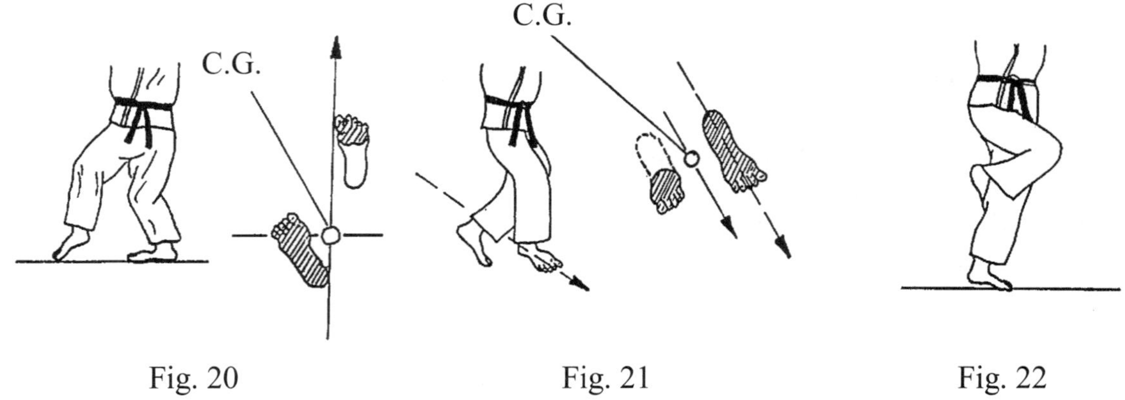



Fig. 20                    Fig. 21                    Fig. 22

Photo 13

Photo 14

Photo 15

## 5 - Fighting stances (Kumite Dachi)

Any natural, basic or varied stances can be converted into a fighting stance.  The main difference is created by positioning the legs closer to each other, so the supporting polygon is reduced for better mobility which is the main requirement for better fighting.  The exception is the Cat-Leg Stance where the legs can be moved wider apart.  Kumite Dachi can be converted into Kihon Dachi for better stability and for better confidence.

# 2.2.  *FOOT  AND  BODY MOVEMENTS*

### Shifting - Turning (Tai Sabaki) and Walking (Shintai)
(See Figs. 23 and 24;   Photos 1 to 12;   Diagrams I. and II. and Diagrams "A", "B", "C", "D")

Foot and body movements are very important factors not just in Karate, but in any other sport.  In Karate, foot and body movements are vital apsects, especially in fighting.  They are used for approaching the opponent with the intention of attack, counterattack or distancing from the opponent by simple stepping back, aside or moving around the opponent to be safe.

Foot and body movements require a good balance and a sense of coordination.  If the balance is poor, the coordination of the techniques, power and speed of execution, will suffer.  Changing the direction of movement from right to left, from front to back, or any other direction, requires a great deal of speed from the athlete.

Body turnings are especially important in defense to create a good avoidance position from the opponent for a better counterattack possibility.  Body turnings are used largely in throwing techniques as well.

## Body shifting - Turning (Tai Sabaki)

Body turning or stepping can be executed mainly in eight directions:

1. Front (Mae) or North
2. Diagonally right front (Migi Naname Mae) or North East
3. Right side (Migi Yoko) or East

4. Diagonally left front (Hidari Naname Mae) or North West
5. Left side (Hidari Yoko) or West
6. Diagonally right back (Migi Naname Ushiro) or South East
7. Back (Ushiro) or South
8. Diagonally left back (Hidari Naname Ushiro) or South West

See Diagram I. This explains the stepping process just when the left leg moves and the Karateka stands in a Shizentai position towards North. This diagram shows the motions, when the left leg steps forward pointing North - A; to North West - A1; to the side to West - A2; back to the South West - A3; or straight back to South - A4. This diagram doesn't show, just a very little pivot action (if made) by the right foot which is considered stationary in this type of foot movement.

While this step is executed with the left leg with a linear motion, the shoulders remain approximately in the same position, or turned just slighlty, but insignificantly, forward or backward to the left side. (See also Fig. 23 for shoulders position during Diagram I.)

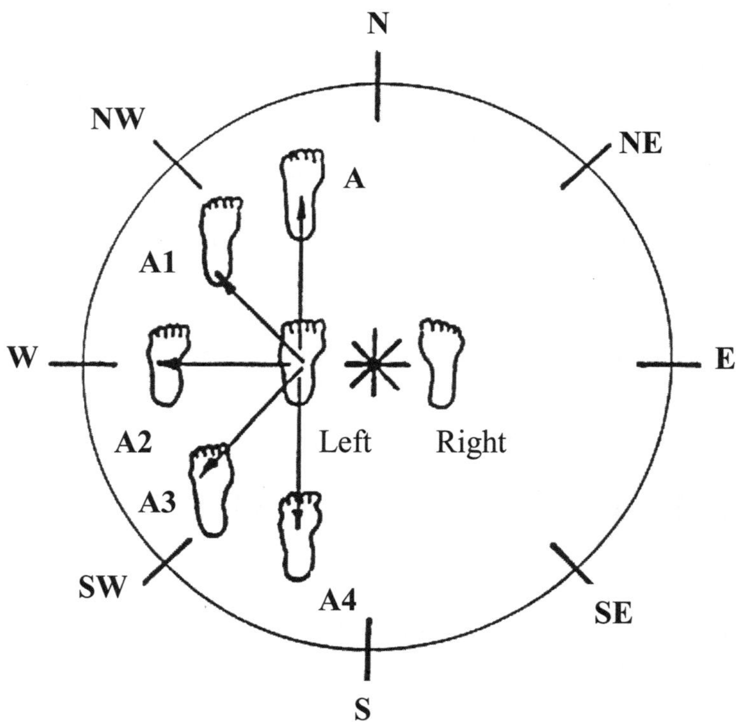


Diagram I.

Left shoulder position while the described steps occured in Diagram I.

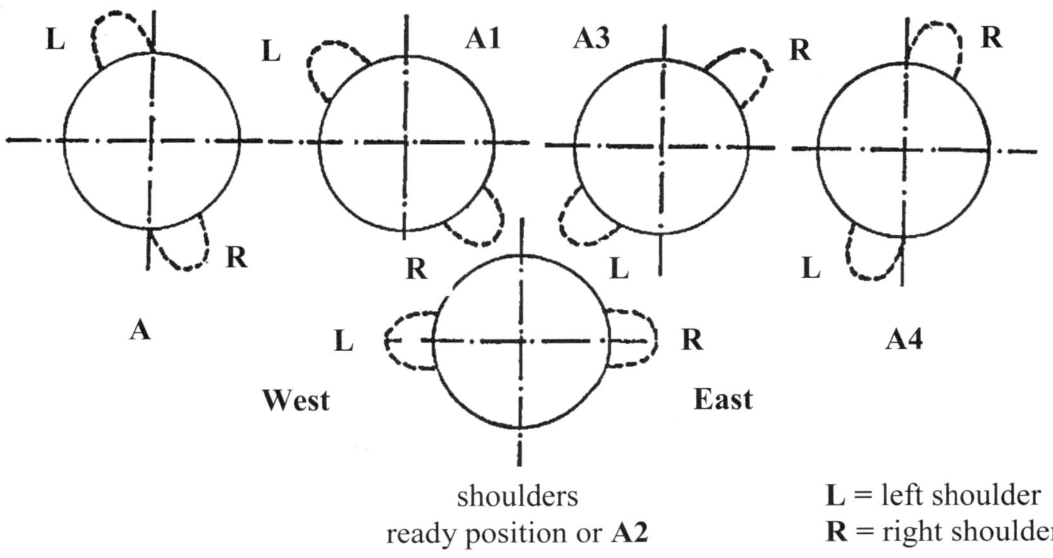


Fig. 23

See Diagram II.  It shows body shifting - turning motion.  For this type of body turning the basic position is the Shizentai to the North.  The turning motions are described, the left leg is making the major step, turning by moving the foot from one spot to another and the right foot pivoting in the same spot or slightly moving away.

In position **B** it shows the left foot moving with an arch backwards to the **SE** and the right foot just pivoting 45 degrees angle with the heel.

In **B1**, the position shows the left foot moved to the **E** and the right foot pivoting 90 degrees angle with the heel.

In **B2**, the position shows the left foot moved to the **NE** with a much larger circle and the right foot now leaving the posted position not just pivoting but moving too.  The body is now directed to the **SW**.

In **B3**, the position shows the whole body turned from the **N** to the **S** 180 degrees angle and the right foot moving with a bigger arch to the left.

(See also Fig. 24 for shoulders position during Diagram II.)

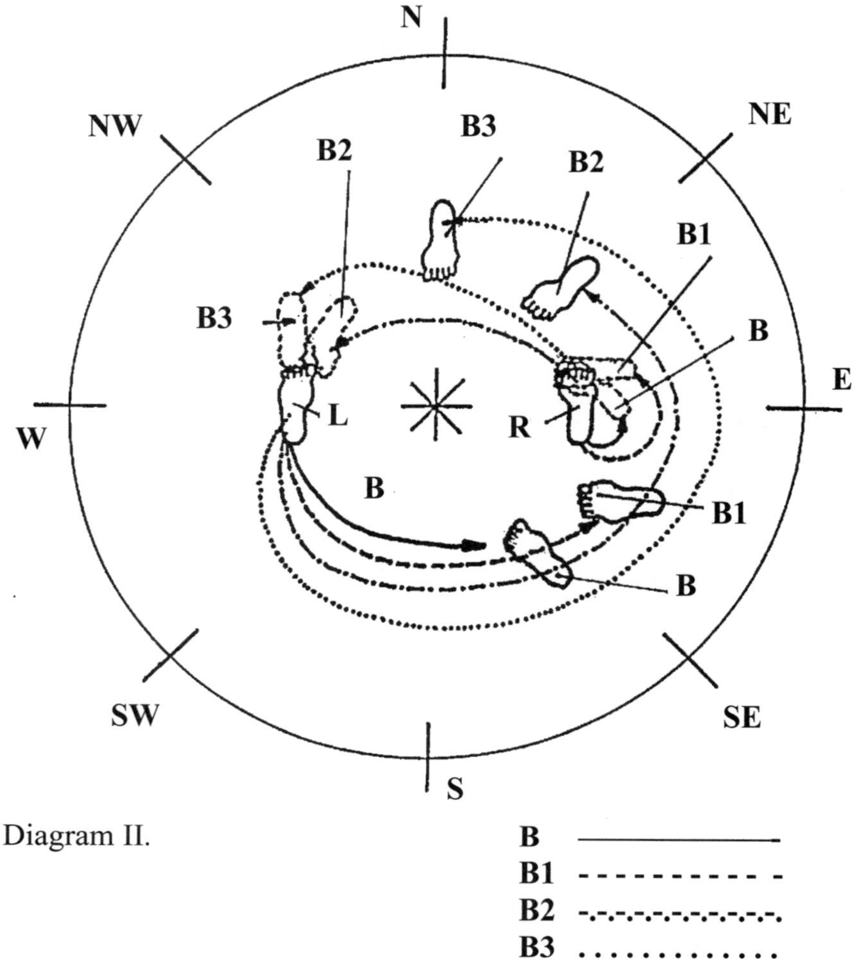


Diagram II.

B ——————
B1 - - - - - - - - - -
B2 -.-.-.-.-.-.-.-.-.-.
B3 . . . . . . . . . . . . .

Shoulders position while the described turnings occured:  Diagram II.

Step **"B"**     Step **"B1"**   Step **"B2"**
NE       SE-N     SW-NE

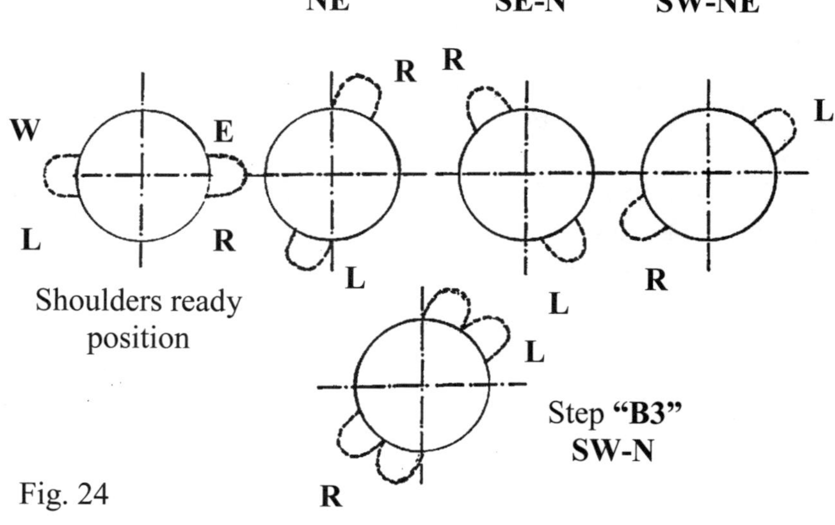


Fig. 24

We just described the stepping - turning actions, when one leg, particularly the left, makes the step or turning, and the right just pivots, or slightly turns.  It is well known that in fighting, complex shifting and turnings happens more than simple one leg shifting.

The following will describe two leg actions, with stepping or turning, which are used in avoiding the attack and moving away from the range of action.

See Diagram **"A"**.  Tori on the left facing to the East and Uke on the right facing to the West, they are both in a right fighting position (Migi Mae Seishan Dachi).  Tori executes a cross leg stepping front leg kick (Surikomi Migi Mae Geri), Uke slides backward to the left to South East, holding the same position and blocking the kick (Photo 1 & 2).

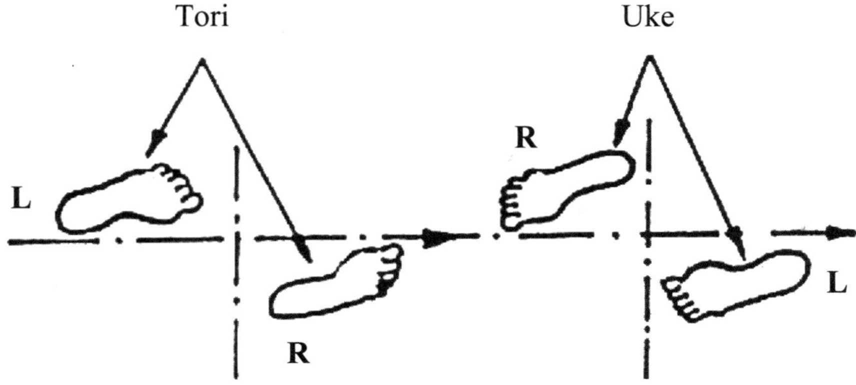


First sequence - the positions

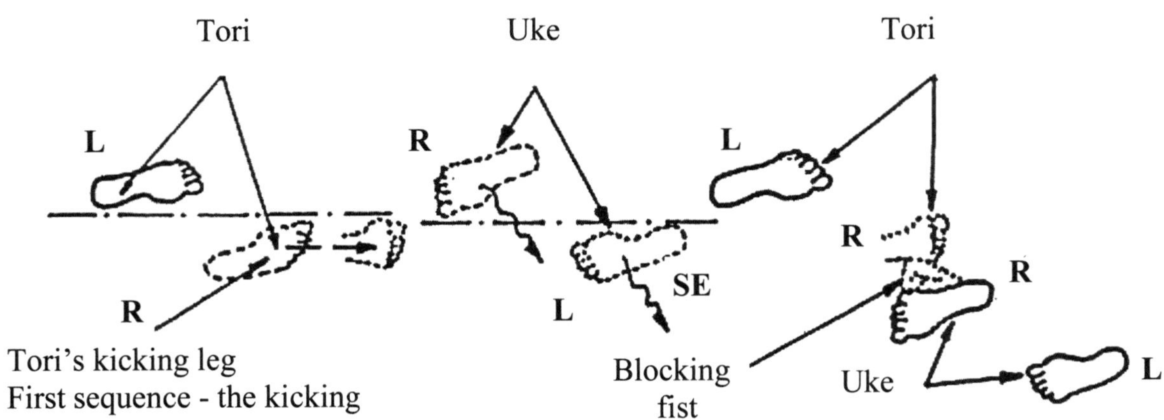


Second sequence - the Uke's body shifting and
blocking

Diagram **"A"**

Photo 1

Photo 2

See Diagram **"B"**. Same position as in Diagram **"A"**. Tori attacks with a Surikomi Migi Jun Zuki at Jodan level. Uke slides forward in the same position and to the right North West, blocking the punch (Photo 3).

See Diagram **"C"**. Tori is in a right position, Uke is in a left position. Tori attacks with a Hidari Jun Zuki. Uke steps back with his left leg just behind his right leg. Tori finishes his attacks to Uke's face and Uke now blocking the attack with his palm or fist and, at the same time, stepping out to the right North West with his right leg (Photo 4, 5 & 6).

See Diagram **"D"**. Both Uke and Tori are in right position. Tori attacks with Hidari Jun Zuki Jodan. Uke maintains the right position, but moves out just a little with his right foot and moves more with his left leg with an arch motion outside to the right, almost in the same way as seen in Diagram II., motion **B**. Because of this action of side stepping with the right and turning with the left, Uke is practically out of range of the action and he can easily counterattack.

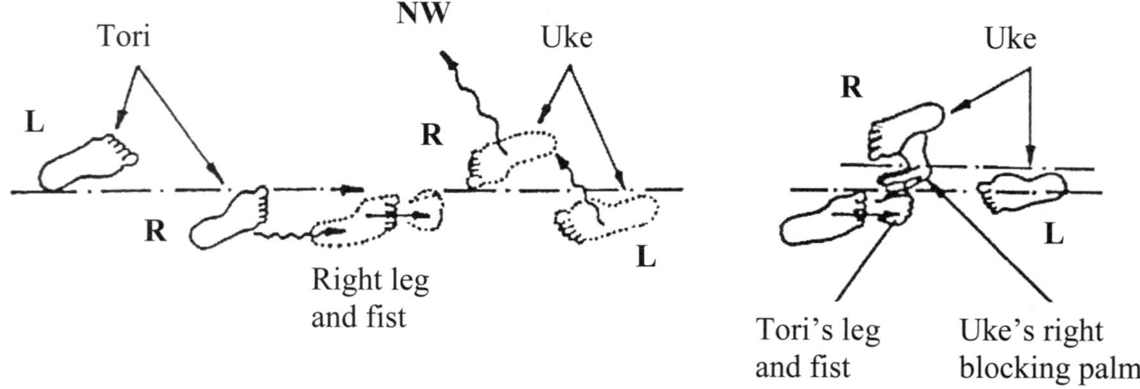


Diagram **"B"**

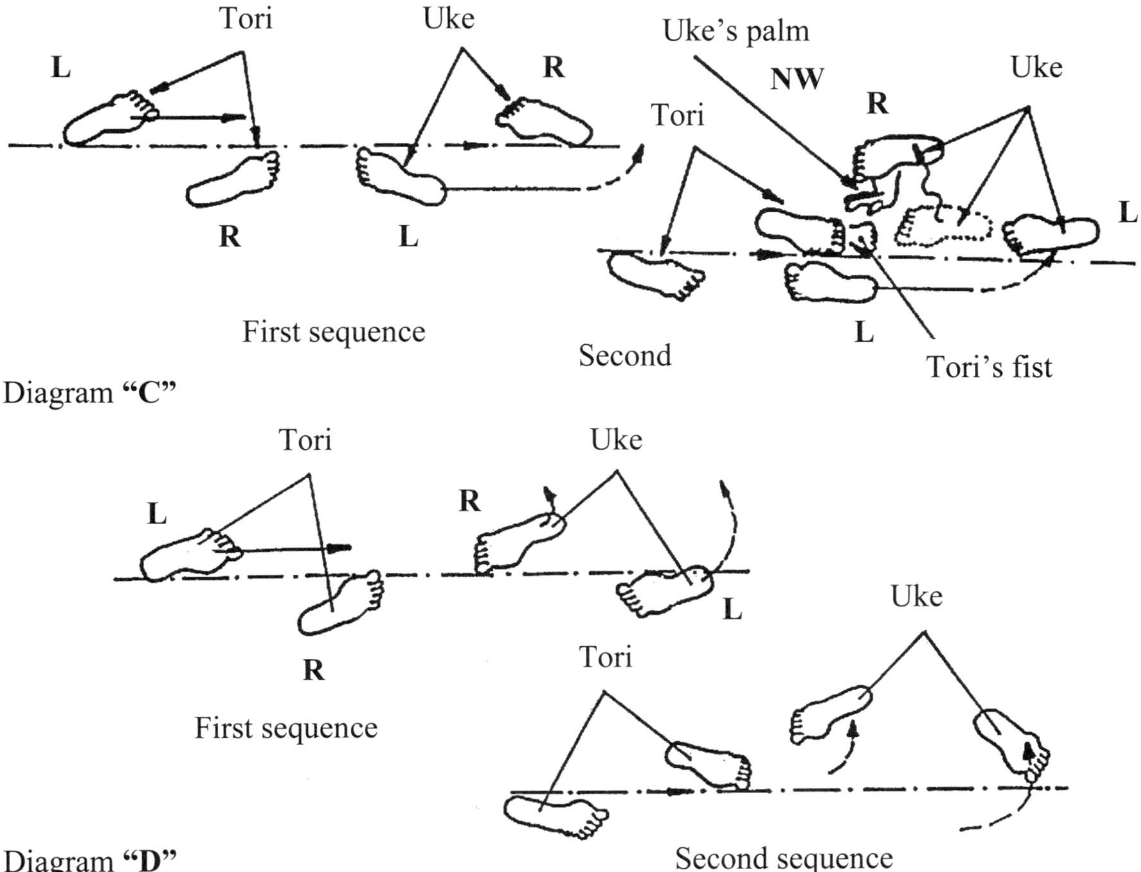



Diagram **"C"**



Diagram **"D"**

Photo 3

Photo 4

Photo 5

Photo 6

# Walking (Shintai)

Walking in Karate is different than walking on the street.  On the street you can lift up your toes from the ground when you move the leg forward or backward.  In Karate and also in Judo, Aikido etc. or martial arts in general you never lift up the toes from the ground.  During stepping motion the moving leg's toes must be in contact at all times with the ground by sliding and lifting up the heel.

Generally there are 3 kinds of walking in Karate:

1.  Normal stepping (Ayumi Ashi), in which the rear leg moves forward holding the toes on the ground (Photo 7, 8 & 9).
2.  Crossed leg stepping (Suri Komi Ashi) (Photo 10, 11 & 12).
3.  Added leg stepping (Tsugi Ashi), not illustrated.  Assume that you are with the left leg in front.  Move the right leg close to the left, then move forward your left leg - repeat again.

Photo 7

Photo 8

Photo 9

Photo 10

Photo 11

Photo 12

# *2.3.  BODY EVASION (Kawashi)*

Body evasions are used to avoid an attack, either because it is more preferable than a block, or just because the block was too late.  That is why a dodging action with the head, with the torso or with the whole body, can be used instead of a complete block.  Body evasions look like body shiftings or even stepping, but in reality there is a big difference between the two types of actions.

Body shifting requires mostly leg moving actions but, on the other hand, body evasions does not require stepping actions, but rather the whole body or the head is usually leaning backwards, sidewards, downwards etc.

**Leaning sideways (Yoko Furimi)**

You are attacked with a punch to the face, you are in Migi Fudo Dachi.  To avoid the attack, shift your weight to the left leg back, assume an Ushiro Zenkutsu Dachi and lean your body to the left.

**Leaning backwards (Ma Sori Mi)**

You are attacked by a side kick to the face, you are in Migi Zenkutsu Dachi.  To avoid the attack, simly take a Hidari Kokutsu Dachi and lean back a little bit.

### Rotation of the trunk (Hineri Hanmi)

Assuming you are in a Shizentai position and a punch or a straight kick comes to your stomach, you simply twist your body in order to avoid the attack.

### Squatting (Otoshi Mi)

This technique can be used effectively against a tall opponent and against high kicks. You simply sink your body to the ground in order to avoid the attack.

### Jumping (Tobi Mi)

You are attacked by a long stick against your leg and so you jump up in order to avoid the attack.

Professor Arus' Aikido master Juo Iwamoto 4th Dan (1975-1976)

# 3.  NATURAL WEAPONS OF KARATE
(See Figs. 25 to 44-7)

Practically any hard part of the body can be used as a natural weapon.  Usually the edge of the bones are conditioned and strengthened to be used for attacks as well as for defense. Generally, there are about forty well known natural weapons used by Karateka and these are classified in 3 large categories:

**1.  Arm weapons    2.  Leg weapons    3.  Head weapon**

## 1.  Arm weapons:

**a.  Closed hand (Ken)**

1 - Normal fist (Seiken) (Fig. 25)

Fold the second and the third phalanges of your fingers together then clench them into your palm, the thumb will press on the second phalange of your index and middle fingers.  On impact squeeze your fist, tighten your wrist and put your strength and mind into it.  The Seiken is considered the basic and most important fist position for attack in almost any Karate style.  In any fighting position the Karateka's fists are clenches into the Tate or Ura (Gyaku Ken) positions, (See descriptions on Tate Ken or Gyaku Ken) and, when the attack occurs, then the fist will be twisted into a Seiken position.  This twisting action gives an extra power to the attacking fist.  The attack is done by the middle and forefinger knuckles (2nd and 3rd metacarpal bones).

2 - Vertical fist (Tate Ken) (Fig. 26)

In the right vertical fist position, the palm side is towrds the left.  This type of fist has more pushing power than the Seiken, which has more snapping power.  The radius and ulna bones are parallel so the joint of the wrist is in a normal position.  In the Seiken position the wrist is oversolicited, because the radius and the ulna are in a twisted "X" position.

3 - Reverse fist (Gyaku Ken) (Fig. 27)

The fingers are facing up and the elbow is bent.  This type of fist attack is used for short attacks (uppercut) to the stomach or chin.

4 - Hammer fist (Tettsui, Kentsui) (Fig. 28)

The outside edge of the fist is used for attack.

5 - Back fist (Uraken, Riken) (Fig. 29)

The base knuckles are used as a weapon.

6 - Hei Ken (Fig. 30)

The part of the phalanges and the base of the palm are used for attack.  The vital point to attack is mainly the ear, nose, heart, and nape.

7 - Four finger knuckle fist (Hiraken) (Fig. 31)

Uses the middle joints of the four fingers.  This is a very sharp weapon, basically used to attack the base of the neck or nose.

8 - One finger knuckle fist (Ippon Ken) (Fig. 32a, 32b & 32c)

Fig. 32a - With forefinger (Hitosashi Ippon Ken),  Fig. 32b - With middle finger (Nakadaka Ippon Ken),  Fig. 32c  With thumb (Oyayubi Ippon Ken)
The Ippon Ken weapons are usually used against bony surfaces and against nerve centers, such as base of the nose, temple, neck, base of the palm, ribs etc.

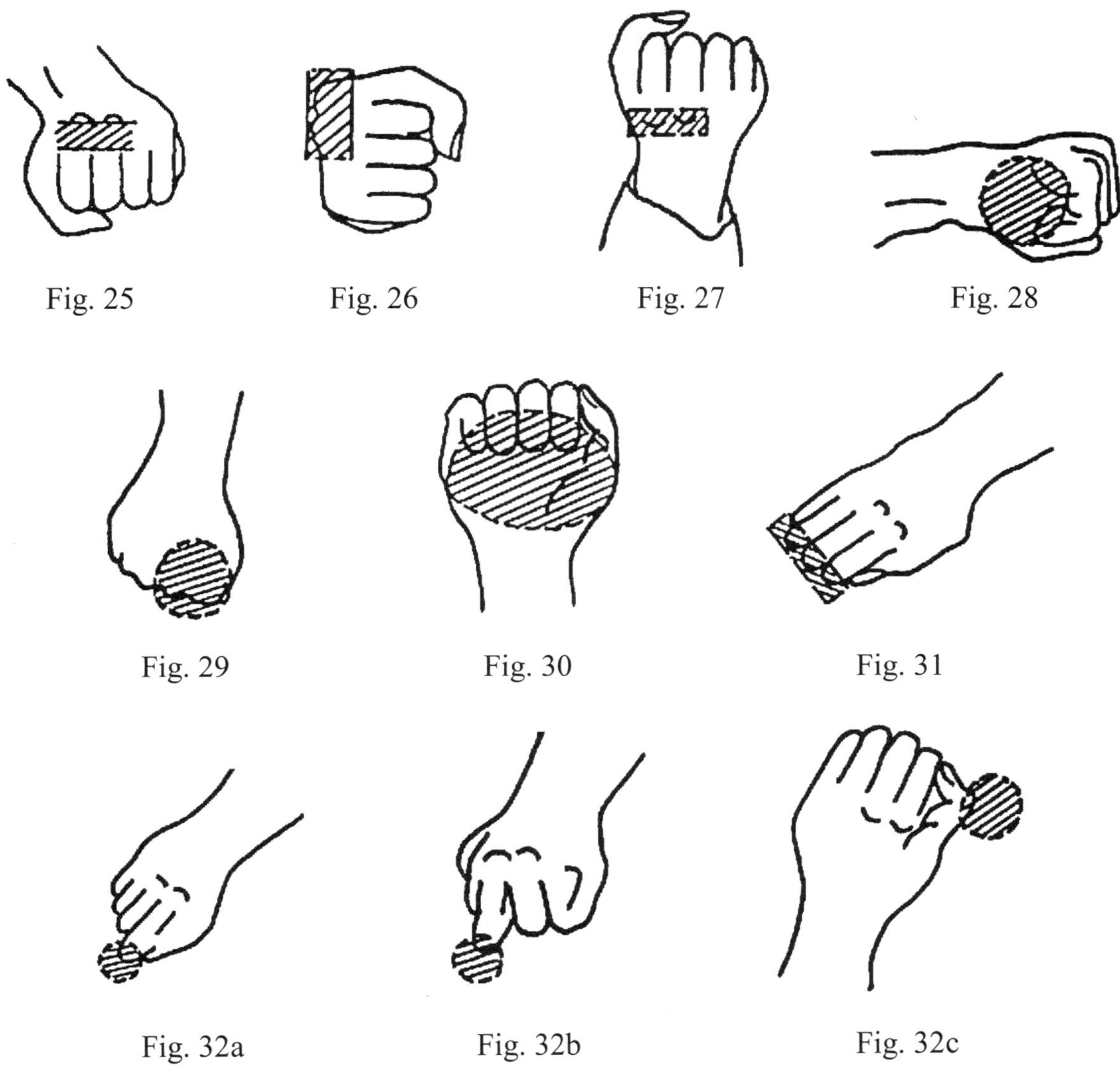

Fig. 25          Fig. 26          Fig. 27          Fig. 28

Fig. 29          Fig. 30          Fig. 31

Fig. 32a          Fig. 32b          Fig. 32c

## b.  Open hand (Kaishu or Kaite)

1 - Knife hand (Shuto or Tegatana) (Fig. 33)

The four fingers are straightened and the thumb bent, pressing it on the inside edge of the hand on the forefinger.  The attack is made with the edge of the palm but not the part of the little finger.  Shuto is used in any direction and against almost any surface.  It can also be used as a block.

2 - Ridge hand (Haito) (Fig. 34)

Contact is made with the inside edge of the palm.  The thumb is bent and pressed against the little finger.  This weapon is used in a circular motion and it is very effective.

3 - Back of the hand (Haishu) (Fig. 35)

Here the back side of the open hand is used.  The fingers are extended and joined together.  Attacks are made against the nose, temple and ears.

4 - Palm heel (Teisho or Shotei) (Fig. 36)

The wrist is bent upward and back; the second phalange of the fingers must be bent. The attack is made with the heel of the palm.  Attacks can be made straight with a pushing motion (Tsuki), or circular motion (Uchi), against the nose, chin, ear, solar plexus, ribs, groin and also they can be used for blocks.  This is an extremely effective weapon.

5 - Open hand (Hirate) (Fig. 37)

Practically, the palm is used for attack in a similar way as the Haishu.

6 - Spear hand (Nukite) (Fig. 38a, 38b & 38c)

Fig. 38a - Yonhon Nukite - All the fingertips are used except the little finger and thumb. Attacks are made against neck, chest, abdomen etc.

Fig. 38b - Nihon Nukite - The fingertips of the index and middle fingers are used for attack and usually against the eyes in a very serious life threatening situation.

Fig. 38c - Ippon Nukite - The fingertip of the index finger is used for attack against one eye.

7 - Bear hand (Kumade) (Fig. 39)

All the fingertips are bent.  The attacking surface includes the fingers and the palm surface.  Usually it is used against the ears.

8 - Eagle hand (Washide) (Fig. 40)

All fingertips are joined at one point.

9 - Toho or Hirabasami (Fig. 41)

The index finger and the thumb form an arch.

10 - Bent wrist (Kakuto or Koken) (Fig. 42)

The wrist is bent.

11 - Ox jaw hand (Seyriuto) (Fig. 43)

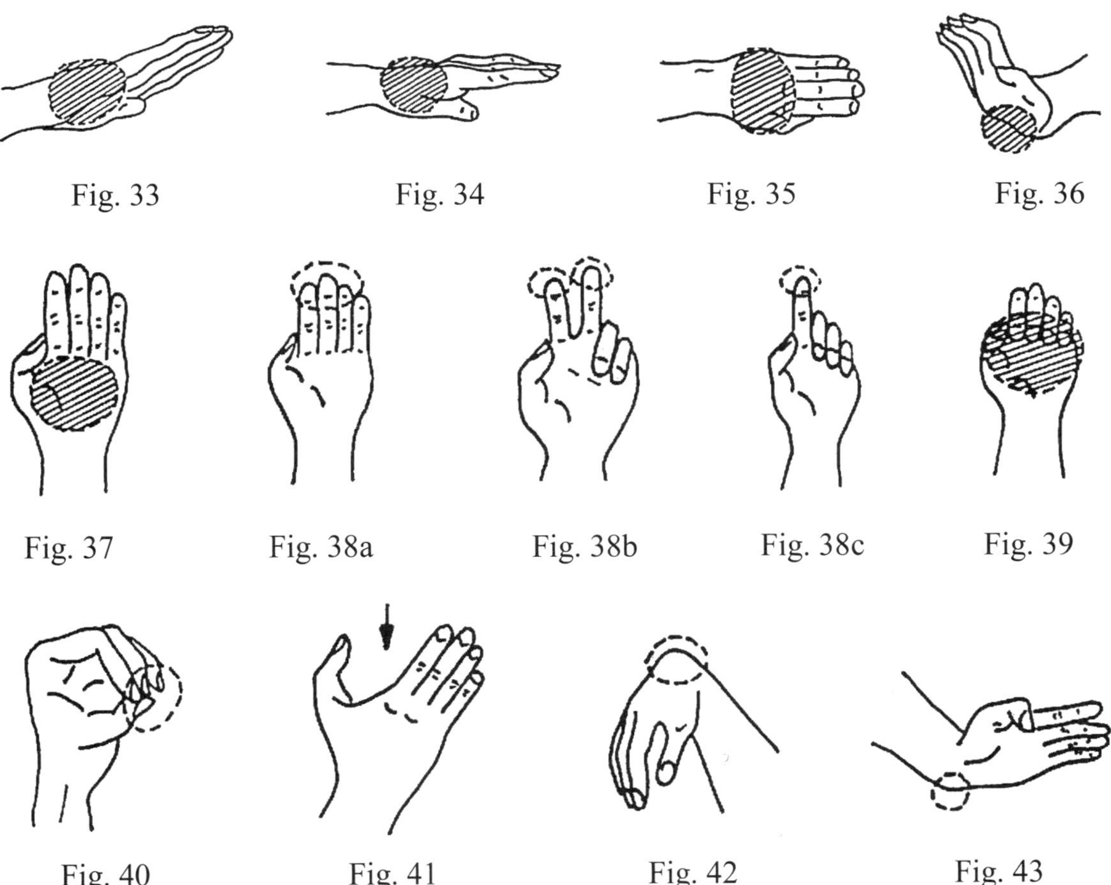

Fig. 33          Fig. 34          Fig. 35          Fig. 36

Fig. 37          Fig. 38a          Fig. 38b          Fig. 38c          Fig. 39

Fig. 40          Fig. 41          Fig. 42          Fig. 43

### c. Forearm (Wan or Kote)

Usually the forearm is used for blocks, but it can also be used for attacks against the neck, face, ear etc.  Usually the outside forearm (Gaiwan), inside forearm (Naiwan) and the back of the forearm (Haiwan) are used for attacks as well as for defense.

### d. Elbow (Empi or Hiji)

The elbow attack is called Empi Uchi or Hiji Ate.  The elbow is the second strongest natural weapon after the knee.  The elbow can be used in attack with a circular motion (Mae or Mawashi Empi Uchi); upward motion to the front (Age Empi Uchi); side (Yoko Empi Uchi); backward (Ushiro Empi Uchi); downward (Otoshi Empi Uchi) and can be used against any part of the human body.

## 2. Leg weapons:

1 - Ball of the foot (Koshi or Yosokutei) (Fig. 44-1)

The toes are bent upward and the ball of the foot is used in a straight or circular attack against the solar plexus, ribs, groin, kidneys, face etc.

2 - Sole of the foot (Teisoku or Sokutei) (Fig. 44-2)

Because this part of the foot is soft, it is used more for sweeping and blocking.

3 - Bottom of the heel (Kakato) (Fig. 44-3)

The foot is in the dorsiflexed position.  Attacks are made forward to the stomach, to the face, backward to the opponent's stomach, or downward on the instep of the opponent.

4 - Back of the heel (Ushiro Kakato) (Fig. 44-4)

It is used with a circular kicking motion to the temple, ribs, stomach etc.

5 - Sword foot or edge of the foot (Sokuto) (Fig. 44-5)

The outside edge of the foot and the heel is used for front, side, and back attacks to the neck, face, stomach, ribs, knees and shins.

6 - Instep (Haisoku) (Fig. 44-6)

Contact is made with the instep.  The ankle and the toes must be kept straight.  Attacks are made to the face, stomach and groin.

7 - Spear foot (Tsumasaki) (Fig.  44-7)

The end of the toes are used to attack the solar plexus, ribs, groin and neck.

8 - Knee (Hiza or Hittsui)

## 3.  Head weapon:

Another weapon that can be used for attack is the head with the forehead (Hitai) or backside of the head (Ryokado).

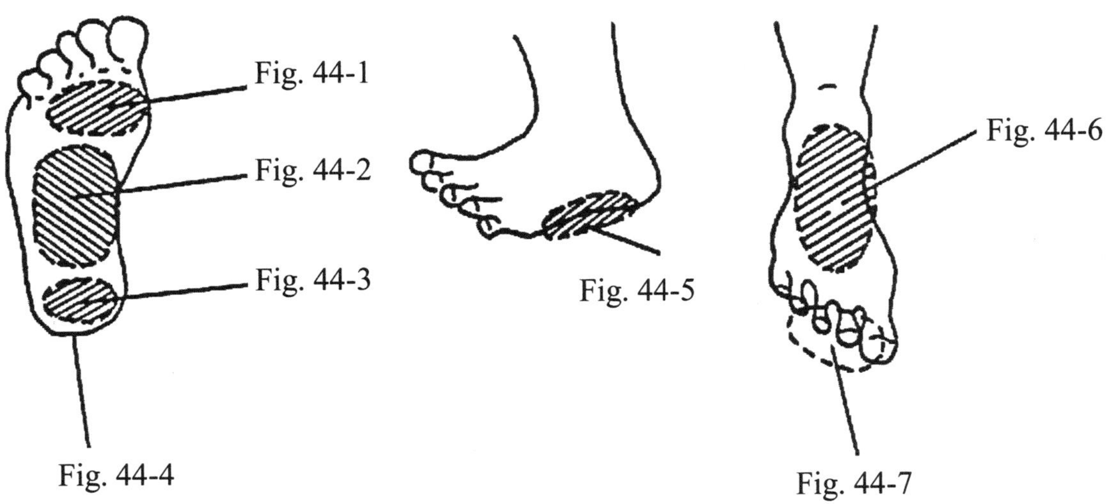

# 3.1.  *VITAL POINTS (Kyusho)*
(See Figs. 45, 46, 47)

The natural weapons of Karate, which were described previously, are used against vital points which can actually cause the loss of consciousness, or death, when the strike has sufficient power.  If the blow is not powerful, or the natural weapon is used incorrectly, or the opponent is extremely well built, then sometimes unconsciousness or death do not occur.

Attacking soft vital points as heart, liver, kidney, spleen, solar plexus can cause unconsciousness, or death, from the combined action of destroyed blood vessels, tissues and by the disconnection of the normal function of the central nervous system (6).

When attacking hard vital points (surfaces of the bones), such as the temple, base of the nose, sternum (xiphoid process), ribs, top of the head, knee cap etc. severe pain, loss of consciousness, or death, will occur mainly from the shock to the central nervous system, because the vital organs, such as the brain, lungs and others are protected by the bone armour system.

It is impossible to classify exactly the combined destroying effect because it depends on many combined factors described above.

Head - Vital points
Fig. 45

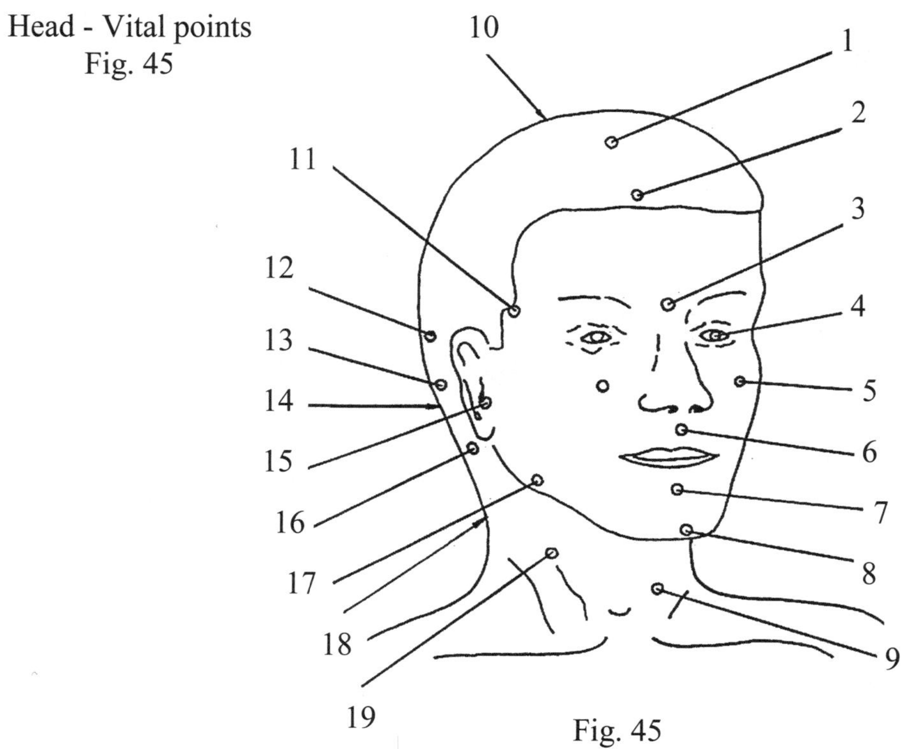


Fig. 45

Head - Vital points

| *Situated* | *Japanese terminology* |
| --- | --- |
| 1 - Bregma | - Tendo |
| 2 - Frontal bone | - Tento |
| 3 - Frontal and nasal bone insertion | - Choto or Uto |
| 4 - Eye ball | - Gansei |
| 5 - Zygomatic bone | - Seidon |
| 6 - Base of the nose | - Kodo or Myojo |
| 7 - Superior portion of the mandible | - Gekon |
| 8 - Mandible | - San Ming in Chinese |
| 9 - Hyoid bone (Adam's apple) | - Hichu |
| 10 - Fonticulus posterior | |
| 11 - Temple | - Kasumi or Ryomo |
| 12 - Point behind the ear | |
| 13 - Point behind the ear | |
| 14 - Base of the cranium (1st vertebra) | - Kochu |
| 15 - Ear | - Mimi |
| 16 - Hollow point of mastoid process | - Dokko |
| 17 - Mandible's angle | - Mikazuki |
| 18 - 3rd and 4th cervical vertebra | - Keichu |
| 19 - Carotid artery | - Murasame or Shofu |

Front part of the body
Vital Points
Fig. 46

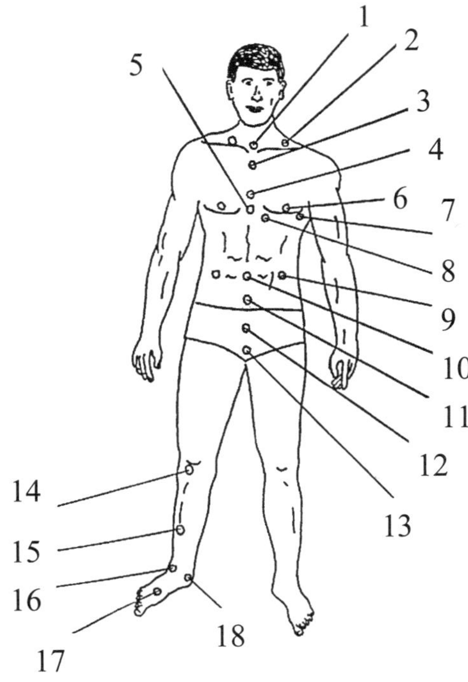


Fig. 46

## Front part of the body - Vital points

| *Situated* | *Japanese terminology* |
|---|---|
| 1 - Base of the neck | - Sonu |
| 2 - Clavicle bone | - Sakotsu |
| 3 - Sternum (Manubrium) | - Chudan or Danchu |
| 4 - Sternum (Xiphoid process) | - Chudan or Kyototsu |
| 5 - Solar plexus | - Kyosen |
| 6 - Pectoralis muscle | - Ganka |
| 7 - Between 5th and 6th ribs | - Kyoei |
| 8 - Cardiac plexus | - Ganchu |
| 9 - The end of false ribs (Costae spuriae) | - Denko or Tchuin in Chinese |
| 10 - Pit of the stomach | - Suigetsu |
| 11 - Hypogastrium | - Myojo |
| 12 - Pubis bone | |
| 13 - Testes | - Kinteki |
| 14 - Patella (Knee cap) | - Hiza Kansetsu |
| 15 - Tibia bone | - Kokutsu |
| 16 - Ankle | - Kori |
| 17 - Os Metatarsus | - So In in Chinese |
| 18 - Os Calcis | - Uchikurobushi |

Back part of the body
Vital Points
Fig. 47

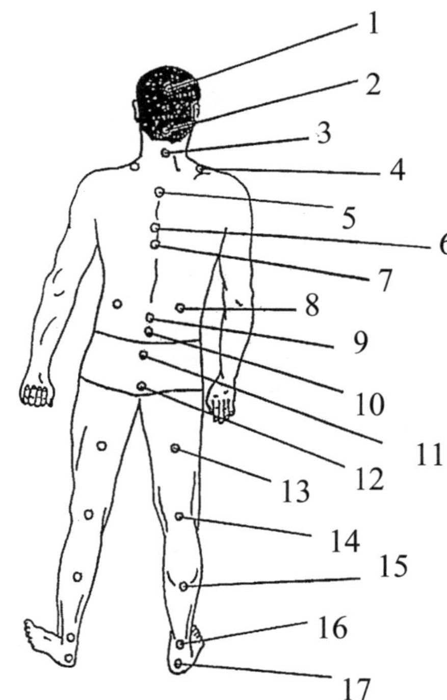


Fig. 47

Back part of the body - Vital points

| *Situated* | *Japanese terminology* |
| --- | --- |
| 1 - Fonticulus posterior | |
| 2 - First vertebra | - Kochu |
| 3 - 3rd and 4th Cervical vertebra | - Keichu |
| 4 - Trapezius muscle | |
| 5 - 7th Cervical vertebra | - Soda |
| 6 - 5th Dorsal vertebra | - Katsusatsu |
| 7 - 7th Dorsal vertebra | - Tche Lang in Chinese |
| 8 - Kidneys | - Hizo |
| 9 - 12th Dorsal vertebra | - Tsie Tsri in Chinese |
| 10 - 1st Lumbar vertebra | - Kodenko |
| 11 - 4th Lumbar vertebra | - Kodenko |
| 12 - Coccyx (Sacrum bone) | - Bitei |
| 13 - Sciatic nerve | - Ko Inazuma |
| 14 - Popliteal space | - Shitsu Kansetsu |
| 15 - Gastrocnemius or Soleus muscle | - Sobi |
| 16 - Achilles tendon | - Akiresuken |
| 17 - Heel bone | |

# 4.  HAND - ARM TECHNIQUES
## (Te Ude Waza)

# 4.1.  PUNCHING TECHNIQUES
## (Tsuki Waza)

The punching techniques are executed usually with the normal position of the fist (Seiken) with a thrusting motion.  It can be a linear but also a circular motion.  It is very important in the execution for a Tsuki, that your whole body mass be activated, but especially the hips.  Before starting the execution of a punch, your whole body should be in a relaxed position.  On impact your fist must be rotated and clenched and also your forearm, arm, shoulder, abdomen, side of your body, hip and leg muscles must be contracted.

The fist rotation should be done as late as possible, but not when the impact occurs. After the contact has been made, your entire body must be relaxed again.

## The application principles of Tsuki Waza

### Fist rotation

When you execute a vertical fist punch (Tate Ken Zuki) the biceps muscles are contracted more than the triceps muscles.  This means that your fist was rotated 90 degrees angle.

Because your triceps muscles have a more important role and effect in pushing, you should rotate the fist 180 degrees angle and, at this time, the triceps muscles will be more contracted than the biceps muscles (7).  By rotating the fist 180 degrees angle the punch will have a more destroying effect.

Rotate the fist at the last moment for greater penetration power and also twist the forearm muscles, in order to unify them into one weapon like a spear.

## Body rotation

A great majority of the dynamic forces utilized in Karate techniques are generated by rotating the body, the shoulders and especially the hips.  It is not uncommon in other sports and fighting art forms, such as Karate, that strength, derived from hip rotation, is essential for stronger offensive and defensive techniques.

The stomach muscles and the body's lateral muscles play a very important role in the rotation of the hips.  A well developed abdominal region tends to support the trunk of the body, enabling one to withstand the shock of the applied techniques.  The thigh muscles also play a major role in smooth and powerful hip rotation.  The thigh muscles, not only aid the rotation of the hips, but also aid in the supporting of the hip bones and pelvic region.  These muscles, when properly developed, will lend greater driving power to the hips, which also will result in a more powerful Karate technique.

By rotating the hips, the power generated travels to the spine which acts as a stabilizing mechanism and a shock absorber.  The power generated continues on to the chest and arm muscles and, finally, to the fist for a more powerful result.

To avoid losing the power of the hips in the rotation of the body, emphasis should be placed in moving the hip first.  The hips, being the slowest part of the body, at the same time are the strongest (rotating) parts of the body.  Reaction-force is also applied to Karate techniques by body - hip rotation, by pressing hard against the floor with the rear leg, while at the same time driving the hip forward.

***Important points to remember which affect hip rotation:***

- Maintaining the correct - vertical posture throughout the rotation.
- Turning the shoulders at the same time that the hips are turned.
- Rotating the hips on the same horizontal line.
- Rotating the hips in one continuous motion and on the same level.
- Twisting the thigh of the rear leg until the front surface is pointing forward.

## Body vibration

On certain occasions, there arises a need for hip oriented power without the time consuming gesture of full hip rotation.  This almost always occurs when delivering multiple techniques, in either defensive or offensive postures.  This slight hip movement is referred to as "Hip vibration" and is the most difficult of hip power to master.

In physiology it is known that any movement initiated within the body requires first a nerve impulse that reaches the muscle fibers.  In the muscle fibers the impulses initiate a chemical reaction that results in the contraction of the fibers.  During this contraction of the muscles, bony attachment are pulled towards each other.  The moving bones act as levers, transmitting energy from the muscle to another object, that may be a body part or an external object.

A limb, or body part, once set in motion by an impulse will continue to move on its own momentum until acted upon by an outside force or an opposing muscle (Newton 1st Law). The muscle, having initiated movement and having developed energy in the body part, then tends to relax. A muscle fiber, which receives a second stimulus while still responding to the first, contracts to a greater degree. If the interval between the first and the second stimulus is of a short duration, then the resulting contraction may triple in degree.

A continuous series of repeated stimuli sent to a muscle evokes a prolonged contraction with a tension as great as four times that of the muscle receiving the first stimulus. The muscle in this case can remain contracted as long as the stimulation continues, or the muscle becomes fatigued.

The example of the straight punch followed by the reverse punch in sequence best describes the use of the hips in utilizing vibration power. Other examples of using vibrations occur in Choku Zuki - multiple punching executions.

For ultimate utilization of counter-rotation and hip vibration power in Karate techniques, the stances and postures play an important role.


### Focusing (Kime)

Execution of any Karate techniques with maximum power in a shortest time is one of the key elements in the effectiveness of our techniques. The key to having a stronger punch is to use as many muscles as possible, especially the muscles around the hips and shoulders. But all the muscles, which will be used for the execution, must be kept in a relaxed position before starting. By pulling back the other hand you can get a momentum effect which helps you twist the body and this twisting causes an acceleration of the punching hand.


## Kinesiological characteristics of punching (Tsuki)

An effective punch is one which has power, speed and maximum energy by the law of dynamics.

### The strength is the product of:

- Entire muscular forces of the body
- Hip rotation momentum
- Body weight
- The retraction of the opposite arm

Gaining a bigger strength is the product of  $F = m.a$

$F$ = force;  $m$ = mass;  $a$ = acceleration

**The speed is the product of:**

- Quality of muscular fibers (especially longer one)
- Quality of muscular fibers, especially the white fibers (Fast Twitch type IIb), because they are for speed; the red fibers are for strength and stamina
- The distance covered by the arms or leg in an execution (generally if the distance is greater then the speed accumulation is greater)
- Increasing the acceleration by rotating the executor limb (fist) as late as possible
- Increasing the acceleration by using the gravity force, techniques executed towards the ground (e.g., Shita Tsuki).

# Punching techniques - Tsuki Waza - Classification:

| Principles of Classification | Biomechanical Movement | Name of Technique |
|---|---|---|
| *One-handed punching techniques:* | | **Tsuki Waza** |
| 1.  Punching with moving away | | |
| – attack executed non-reverse (fist & leg on the same side) | – rectilinear movement (medium & long distance) | Oi Zuke, Jun Zuki, Age Zuki |
| | – rectilinear movement + hip rotation (long & very long distance) | Jun Zuki No Tsukkomi |
| – attack executed reverse (fist & leg on the opposite side) | – by hip rotation (attack direct) | Gyaku Zuki |
| | – rectilinear + body inclination + hip rotation | Gyaku Zuki No Tsukkomi |
| 2.  Punching without moving away | | |
| – attack to medium distance (fist & leg on the same side) | – rectilinear movement (attack direct) | Mae Te Zuki; Tobi Komi Zuki; Kizami Zuki |
| | – rectilinear movement + rotation of the upper body (attack with dodging) | Nagaski Mawashi Zuki |
| 3.  Punching with circular movement | | |
| – attacks can be executed: non-reverse, reverse or any position | – circular by arm rotation (medium distance) | Mawaski Zuki |
| | – hooking by arm rotation (closed distance) | Kagi Zuki |
| | – elbow is bent (short circular motion) | Ura Zuki |

| Principles of Classification | Biomechanical Movement | Name of Technique |
| --- | --- | --- |
| *Two-handed punching techniques:* | | **Morote Tsuki Waza** |
| 1. Attacks on the same level | | |
|    – the leg positions are indifferent | – rectilinear movement | Heiko Zuki |
| | – by scissor movement | Hasami Zuki |
| 2. Attacks are executed on different levels | | |
|    – on Jodan and Chudan level punches are executed in non-reverse/reverse positions | – rectilinear movement | Awase Zuki |
| | – rectilinear movement + arm rotation | Yama Zuki |

# Description of varied punching techniques
(See Figs. 48 to 54 also Photos 1 to 9)


### Straight Punch (Choku Zuki) (Fig. 48)

Assume a natural stance (Shizentai) position.  The left arm is extended in front of the body with the fist closed at the navel level.  The fist has the Seiken position.  The right fist is kept under the right armpit Gyaku Ken position on the right side of the body.  The whole body is in a completely relaxed position.

The right arm starts with a thrusting motion forward punch and, at the same time, the left arm is pulled back.  The right fist starts to twist downward in Seiken position, before punching the opponent's body approximately one fist distance apart.  On impact the right fist and the whole right arm, shoulder and right side of the performer's body is tensed and the left fist now is at the left armpit level with the fingers upwards.  On impact the right fist should be clenched.  This execution is suitable for beginners.

Fig. 48

### Lunge Punch or Stepping Punch (Jun Zuki or Oi Zuki) (Fig. 49 & Photo 1)

From a Hidari Zenkutsu Dachi position, the left arm is extended forward with a closed fist.  The execution of this punch starts with the left foot heel moving to the right 45 degrees angle and then the right leg starting to move forward in a semicircular motion.

The semicircular motion goes forward to the left, then again to the right and to the front. During  stepping, the body must be kept straight.  When the right foot arrives in front, but is not yet set down firmly, the right arm already starts to punch and the left arm is pulled back. Therefore, the right foot must have the contact with the ground with a fraction of a second before the right fist reaches the target.

In the final position, the shoulders are rotated 45 degrees angle with the right shoulder leading slightly forward.  This punch can be executed with Seiken or Tateken.

### Reverse Punch (Gyaku Zuki) (Fig. 50 & Photo 2)

It is executed in a Hidari Zenkutsu Dachi position with the right fist punching Migi Gyaku Zuki.  However, when stepping occurs with the right leg forward, then the left fist punches.  From a Hidari Zenkutsu dachi position with the left arm extended and the right knee slightly bent, the right hip starts to rotate to the left and the right fist with the right shoulder starts to move forward.

On impact the shoulders are parallel with the target, or the right shoulder is in a slightly advanced position in comparison with the left shoulder.  Gyaku Zuki can be executed from other positions as well, for example, Sochin, Sanchin, Hangetsu, Neko Ashi Dachi positions etc.

Fig. 49　　　　　　　　　　　　　　　　Fig. 50

Photo 1　　　　　　　　　　　　　　　Photo 2

**Jumping Punch or Jab (Tobi Komi Zuki or Kizami Zuki)**
(Fig. 51 & Photos 3, 4, 5 and 6)

It is a very fast and powerful punch.  From the Migi Shizentai position, the right forearm starts rising and twisting while the right foot moves forward.  As the punch is executed the left forearm is lifted up, twisted and brought to the middle of the chest.  Both arms are pulled back along with the right foot into Migi Shizentai position.

Fig. 51

Photo 3

Photo 4

Photo 5

Photo 6

**Flowing Round Punch (Nagashi Mawashi Zuki)** (Fig. 52 & Photo 7)

This is a special punch unique to the Sendo-Ryu system. The execution starts as a straight punch, up until the opponent starts to block, then it turns into a round punch with body dodging and shifting, at the same time of execution. This punch can be used as an attack, or as a stopping attack in the attacks of the opponent.

***Flowing Round Punch as an attack***

In Hidari Shizentai position the arms are held down. The left leg starts to slide forward until it reaches the Hidari Zenkutsu Dachi whilst, at the same time, the arms are raised up to the chest level. The left fist is raised up to the face level, and the arm is bent, with the elbow is down. When the left foot arrives in the Hidari Zenkutsu Dachi position, then the left fist executes the punch with a circular motion and the right leg moves to the left approximately in the same line with the left leg making altogether a dodging motion.

Blocks against such an attack are very difficult because the punching arm is moved first straight, then turned into a round execution.

Fig. 52

Photo 7

**Lunge Pushing Punch (Jun Zuki No Tsukkomi)** (Fig. 53 & Photo 8)

This kind of punch is executed like Jun Zuki except, on impact, the punching arm should push forward more, thus inclinating the upper body closer to the opponent.  In the final position, the rear leg and the upper body should be in the same line, therefore creating a 45 degrees angle with the ground.  The attack should occur mainly against the opponent's upper level.

**Reverse Pushing Punch (Gyaku Zuki No Tsukkomi)** (Fig. 54 & Photo 9)

The execution is the same as the Gyaku Zuki execution but, on final impact, the upper body and the rear leg are in the same line.

Fig. 53

Fig. 54

Photo 8

Photo 9

# *4.2. STRIKING TECHNIQUES*
## *(Uchi Waza)*
(See Figs. 55, 56, 57 & Photos 1 and 2)


The striking techniques use a semi-circular motion aimed at the target.  Striking techniques involve the snapping action of the elbow and rely a great deal on the laws of action and reaction for their power.  Punching techniques are more powerful than striking techniques.  However, striking techniques work like baseball pitching techniques.  A ball thrown by a baseball pitcher can reach speeds up to 110-150 km/h.  In punching techniques reaching such speed is not possible.

In order to reach maximum speed and power in striking techniques, the elements of kinetics and biomechanics, such as body twisting, shifting the center of gravity, body weight coordination, snapping the forearm, etc. should be used correctly.


### Back Fist Strike (Uraken Uchi or Riken Uchi)

The back fist strike is one of the fastest striking techniques used in Karate and it is also very effective.  Defense against Uraken Uchi is somewhat easier than against a straight punch even if this strike is 2-3 times faster than a straight punch.  The reason for easier defense is because of the nature of the technique execution.  The striking arm's elbow must be raised up in order to accelerate the strike and therefore this elbow lift is somewhat telegraphic movement that the opponent can see more easily and react upon.


*Uraken Uchi can be executed:*

- In front - Mae Uraken Uchi.
- From an up, to downward motion - Tate or Otoshi Uraken Uchi.
- From a down, to an upward motion - Age Uraken Uchi, usually hits the chin.
- With a circular motion - Mawashi Uraken Uchi, can usually hit the cheek or the ear.

### Front Back Fist Strike (Mae Uraken Uchi) (Fig. 55)

In Migi Shizentai position the arms are held down in a relaxed position.  Both arms with the fists are closed and lifted up to the chest.  The right arm is in front of the left arm, the body twists more to the left, and the right shoulder is almost perpendicular towards the target.  The right elbow is now up to the level of the executor's chin.

The right forearm extends toward the target moving parallel with the ground.  Before reaching the target about four inches away (10 cm), the right fist must be snapped forward for a more devastating effect.  After the strike the arms return down, close to the body, in a relaxed position.  At the time of impact the left foot can pivot backward to the left.

### Hammer Fist Strike (Tettsui or Kentsui Uchi)

This strike is made by using the little finger side of the clenched fist.
- Can be sideward - Yoko Tettsui Uchi.
- Can be vertical - Tate Tettsui Uchi.

### Ridge Hand Strike (Haito Uchi) (Fig. 56)

The strike is made by the opposite side of the knife hand.

There are many other striking techniques:
**Back Hand Strike (Haishu Uchi)**
**Palm Base Strike (Teisho Uchi)**
**Knife Hand Strike (Shuto Uchi)** (Photo 1) or so said Karate chop and this can be Soto or Uchi.
**Elbow Strike (Empi Uchi)** (Fig. 57 & Photo 2) and this can be to the front (Mae Empi Uchi), to the front with the round motion (Mawashi Empi Uchi), to the side (Yoko Empi Uchi), upwards motion (Age Empi Uchi), or downward motion (Otoshi Empi Uchi).

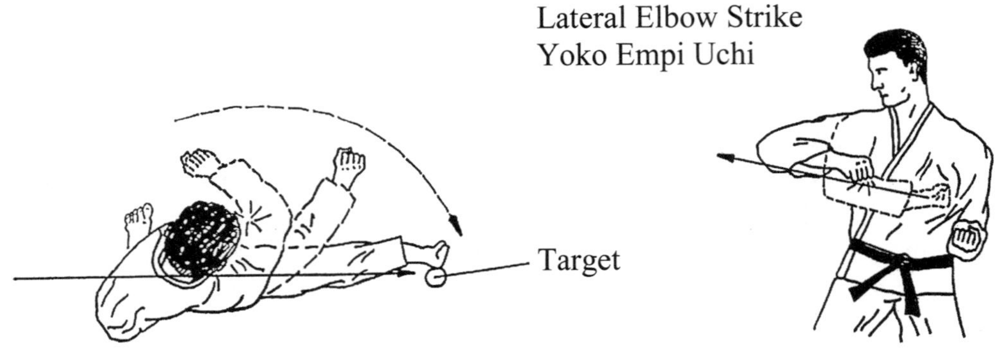



Fig. 55

Fig. 57

Fig. 56

Photo 1

Photo 2

# 4.3.  HAND AND ARM BLOCKING TECHNIQUES  (Te Ude Uke Waza)

(See Figs. 58 to 63 & Photos 1 to 5)

## Technical and general characteristics

In the art of Karate, a well-known important precept is "Karate Ni Sente Nashi", that there is no first attack in Karate (G.Funakoshi).  Therefore, it means that the defending techniques, such as blocking and parries, are very important for any Karateka.

Blocking is a difficult process that requires the anticipation of the opponent's offensive action.  In the process of blocking, every effort must be taken to convert the offensive gestures of the opponent to your advantage.

The power generated in a focused block is sometimes so strong that it discourages any further attack from the opponent.  In essence, "Focused blocks" are attacks.  The concentration of strength of the whole body into a focused block also aids in maintaining proper balance and posture in the event of further attacks.  In some instances retreat is a safer action which can be utilized without blocking.  To succesfully block the opponent's attack, hard and soft techniques must be used alternately.  For example, a hard attack should be blocked with a soft block (parry), absorbed, or simply by using dodging techniques.  After a soft block the counter technique or attack must be hard.

The opponent's arms and legs should be considered, at all times, dangerous weapons, especially when the opponent is visibly strong.  Therefore, hard contact should be avoided as much as possible.  Shifting, sweeping, parrying, or stopping techniques should be used rather than blocking.

Blocks against kicks are a unique feature in comparison with the other fighting sports. The feet and legs can be brought into play, as well as the hands and arms for the purpose of blocking.  But whatever segment is used, every effort should be made to convert the opponent's strength to your advantage and that the blocking segment is not overextended but held ready in preparation for further techniques.

Every effort should be made to minimize openings in your own posture and have a clear mind as to what countermeasures can be used in follow-up.  Balance and posture are of prime concern, serving to render additional force to the blocking technique applied.

The force applied to a block should follow in a certain direction for maximum effectiveness.  The face is protected by blocking from underneath upwards, while the midsection is protected by blocking from the outside inward or viceversa (many times to the face too), and the groin area is protected by blocking below in a downward and outward (or inward) motion.  Forearm rotation lends power to the applied technique and it is a guide ensuring proper deflection away from the body.  After judging your opponent's speed and distance, a block executed too early, or too late, is nothing but wasted effort.

To enhance the power of blocking techniques the hips should be rotated in "Hanmi", approximately in a 45 degrees angle position from the starting position.  An effective block depends on concentrating all body power in the forearm at the moment of impact.

The elbow has a very important role in blockings.  When the elbow is touching, or almost touching, the defender's body, the utilized power for blocking is at the maximum, but this opens the risk for a late counter.  When the elbow is too far from the body, the block is incorrect and weak.  The elbow should be at a distance away from the body, equal to about the width of a fist.  Overblocking results in loss of balance, loss of tension in the side muscles of the body, reduction of body stability, and difficulty in executing follow-up techniques.

The most common part of the body, that is utilized as a blocking area, is the forearm. The surface of the bony part of the forearm, especially the one close to the wrist, can be devastating in blocking but, basically, it is the inner parts (ulna bone side), or outer parts (radius bone side), are usually used as well as the middle surface area of the forearm, or closer to the elbow area.

When the forearm toughens (especially the inner side), it can do devastating blocks (blows) to an opponent's attacking arm or leg and, therefore, discourages further attacks.

Prof. Arus on right, poses with George R. Parulski, Jr., Ph.D. - 8th Dan Hanshi, Vice President of Dai Nippon Seibukan Budo/Bugei Kai, Japan and USA Director / Okazaki Ha Shin Tenshin Shin'yo Ryu Bu Jutsu Renmei.  This photo was taken after the presentation of Sendo-Ryu style on November 14, 1987, where Mr. Parulski, representing Seibukan, acknowledged Sendo-Ryu as a genuine and authentic new Karate style.

# Classification of Blocking Techniques

**I. Arm Blocking Techniques:**

    **I. 1.  One Handed Blocks - I. 1.a.  Blocking by Force**
                                 **I. 1.b.  Blocking by Suppleness**
                                 (parrying, sweeping, hooking)

    **I. 2.  Two Handed Blocks - I. 2.a.  Blocking by Force**
                                   **I. 2.b.  Blocking by Suppleness**
                                 (parrying, sweeping, hooking)

**II.  Leg Blocking Techniques:**

    **II. 1.  Blocking by Suppleness**

## *Consideration about Blocking by Force or Suppleness*

**Blocking by Force**

When the blocking technique is executed with a considerable hitting force against the opponent's arms, or legs, the block must be done with a fraction of a second before the attack reaches the target.

**Blocking by Suppleness**

**1.  Parrying** (Fig. 58)

This kind of block is executed approximately in the same manner as the previous one but, on impact, the defender's body, especially the torso - (shoulders), is rotated towards the blocking line.  Because the torso is rotated towards the blocking line, this block (parry) is considered an absorbed defense.  (Also the contact time is longer).

Speaking about *absorbed blocks* they can be done when the Tori attacks to the stomach, then the Uke lets the attack enter about 50-70 % and, for the remaining %, the Uke simply pulls the stomach in order to avoid the remaining power.  In such a way, the full amount of the shock is dissipated.

### 2. Sweeping (Fig. 59)

Presupposes an earlier contact with the opponent's limbs and the contact time is much longer than in parrying.  The blocking motion is made as a sweeping action and the defender's blocking arm has a retreat action.  The best example is sweeping hand block (Te Nagashi Uke), which is executed with the palm.  This sweeping technique can be combined and executed at the same time with the leg in a sweeping or hooking action (Ko Uchi Gari) - minor inside reap or sweep.  Usually parrying and sweeping techniques are done by open hands.

### 3. Hooking

Hooking techniques involve a rotation of the forearm, from inward to outward, while hooking and pressing the opponent's arm downward.  When executed against a kick the hooking arm is started from outward to inward, blocking and lifting the opponent's leg and then continuing an outward execution, throwing the opponent by lifting his leg and making him lose his balance.

Blocking techniques can also be classified as *hard blocks* which are executed all the time with the fist clenched using the hitting power to eliminate the attackers limb and *soft blocks,* which are executed mainly with the open hand, or sometimes with the fist clenched, which are sweeping or parrying techniques.

Fig. 58

Fig. 59

# Description of major blocking techniques
(Figs. 60 to 63. & Photos 1 to 5)

## I.  Arm Blocking Techniques:
## I. 1.  One Handed Blocks

## I. 1.a.  Blocking by Force

**Rising Block (Jodan Age Uke)** (Fig. 60 & Photo 1)

This block is used against head attacks.  The arms cross at chin height.  The blocking arm moves upwards and the blocking side of the forearm becomes the interior side called Naiwan (the Ulna bone part).  The nonblocking arm is moving downward stabilizing the fist tightly near the chest under the armpit.  The fist of the blocking forearm is tightened along with the abdominal and chest muscles on impact.

The blocking forearm is about 4 inches in front of the forehead, while the fist is higher than the elbow.  (The blocking fist's palm side looks forward.)

**Rising Knife Hand Block or Rising Sword Hand Block (Jodan Shuto Uke)**, is a variation of Jodan Age Uke.  The block is executed with the outside edge of the palm.

**Middle Body Section Inward Forearm Block (Chudan Uchi Ude Uke)** (Fig. 61 & Photo 2)

This block is used against a punch or kick aimed at the chest.  Blocking with the inner edge - Naiwan - of the forearm.  The forearm is bent, raised up in front of the body and making an angle of 100-110 degrees with the upper arm.  The blocking fist is high approximately at face level and at a distance of 16-18 inches away from the face.  The elbow is kept a little bit away from the body.  The upper body is rotated in Hanmi 45 degrees angle, while the blocking arm's shoulder is in front.

The blocking arm starts to move inward and backward a little bit, blocking the opponent's arm with a *snapping motion.*  The blocking arm in the final position is bent about 90 degrees angle and the forearm makes an angle approximately 45 degrees angle with the ground line.

The blocking fist (palm side) is towards the defender's face, while the elbow is about 3-4 inches in front of the body and the muscles around the armpit are tensed, (of course the arm muscles too).  The nonblocking arm at the beginning of the block is in same position as the blocking arm was described before; it is closer to Uke's body and, on blocking, the fist is pulled back and positioned at the hip.  The hip should be rotated in the direction of the block.


**Downward Block (Gedan Uke)** (Fig. 62 & Photo 3)

The block is used against a punch or kick to the abdomen, or lower level, with the wrist and the forearm blocking downward and to the side.  The fist of the blocking arm is about 6 inches away from the thigh of the front leg (Oi Gedan Uke position).


## I. 1.b.  Blocking by Suppleness


**Sweeping Hand Block (Te Nagashi Uke)** (Fig. 59)

This technique has a similar motion as Chudan Uchi Ude Uke, but does not block with the forearm, but with the open palm and the block is made as a sweeping action while the defender's arm does a retreating action during the block.


**Downward Sweeping Block (Gedan Barai)** (Photo 4)

This block is similar to Gedan Uke, but the blocking arm does not block the attacking arm or leg but, instead, uses a sweeping motion.


## I. 2.  Two Handed Blocks


## I. 2.a.  Blocking by Force


**Downward X Block (Gedan Juji Uke)** (Fig. 63 & Photo 5)

This technique is used against kicks, mainly against front kicks, and it is probably the most powerful blocking technique which uses both forearms.  The two forearms form an X, crossing each other and the blocking surfaces are the forearms near the wrists.

In Hidari Zenkutsu Dachi position the two forearms are raised upwards (fists are at the right chest level, the right fist is above the left).  The left forearm starts to block downwards to the left side and it is followed up by the right forearm as a punch execution crossing above the left blocking forearm, with the palm side looking sidewards (towards left).

## I. 2.b.  Blocking by Suppleness

### Two Handed Grasping Block (Morote Tsukami Uke)

Usually the two palms are open and the arms are extended forward in a relaxed position. When an attack occurs, for example  a punch to the middle section, the palms catch the opponent's arm simultaneously, pulling the arm backward - downward towards the left or right side of the defender.  When the Tori attacks with his left arm and the Uke blocks the attack towards his left side then, in this position, the Tori's arm (elbow) can be broken using a technique (Kansetsu Waza).

## II.  Leg Blocking Techniques:

## II. 1.  Blocking by Suppleness

Any leg blocking technique against any arm or leg attack is made only by *blocking suppleness*, except the tapping techniques which can be considered as forms of attack.  Here are a few leg or foot blocking techniques:

### Hooking Ankle Block (Ashi Kubi Kake Uke)

### Circular Sole Block (Mikazuki Geri Uke) etc.

In Kumite we can find just a few blocks that are executed purely.  Generally, the blocks cannot be executed purely, because the executant loses his balance, or starts to use a soft block, which should be immediately converted into a hard block etc.

In Kata we can execute purely every block, but the variety of the blocks are reduced to basic ones.

Fig. 60          Fig. 61          Fig. 62

Fig. 63          Photo 1

Photo 2

Photo 3

Photo 4

Photo 5

# 5.  *LEG  TECHNIQUES (Ashi Waza)*

Leg techniques include kicking techniques (Keri Waza), leg blocking techniques (Ashi Uke Waza), and sweeping - leg throwing techniques (Ashi Harai Nage Waza).

# 5.1.  *KICKING  TECHNIQUES* *(Keri Waza)*

## Technical characteristics

Kicking techniques use the whole of one's body to the maximum.  The hips and body balance are especially of prime importance in effecting maximum power output.  Kicking techniques are two - three times stronger than punching techniques, but they have a lack of balance.  In kicking techniques balance is very important, due to the fact the entire weight of the body has to be supported by one leg while kicking.  The supporting foot must be kept in full contact with the ground and the ankle of the supporting leg must be tensed.  The shock of the kick should be absorbed by the supporting leg, mainly the ankle, knee and the hip.

In a kicking execution the hips can be pushed towards the target (hip progression (8)) especially in front kick execution, or they can be rotated and pushed towards the target in roundhouse kick executions (hip rotation (9) and progression).

In side kick executions, the hips are elevated laterally (abducted (10)) towards the target, and then move back (adducted (11)) to the original starting position.  In all kicking techniques, the knee of the kicking leg should be raised as high as possible, with the knee bent fully, while pointing to the target, with the foot automatically following.  The kicking leg must be withdrawn quickly after completing the kick.  This decreases the probability of your opponent sweeping your supporting foot, or catching the kicking leg.

The bending and lifting of the knee will keep the weight of the kicking leg close to the body, ensuring greater power in the kick.  The supporting leg should remain steady with the knee slightly bent.  This will ensure greater stability while balancing on one leg and increase the potential for absorbing and withstanding the shock when the foot hits the target.  To have effective and powerful kicking techniques, it is necessary to develop strong body muscles, especially those surrounding the abdominal region.

Generally, there are three types of kicks using all areas of the foot, from the tip of the toes to the heel of the foot.

The three types of kick are: *Snap, thrust and striking* kick.  The knee, in all three types, plays an important role.

**Snap kicks (Keage)** depend for their succes on snapping the leg straight from the knee and then back again as quickly as possible.  Once raised, the knee is used as a fulcrum for a semi-circular movement.

**Thrust kicks (Kekomi)** rely on raising the knee first and then thrusting the leg straight using the force of the hip for additional power.

**Striking kicks** may be used for blocking or attacking, and their virtue is flexibility of the whole leg.  Also in striking kicks the knee itself serves as the striking area and can be applied to the front from either an upward motion or a circular motion from the side.

Kicking techniques can be applied to theree different directions: To the front, to the rear, and to the side.  If it is necessary to attack diagonally, then the body must be shifted.  During the kick, the upper body is leaning easily into the kick, sometimes in the same direction as the kicking leg but, most of the times, the leaning is opposite to the kicking leg's direction.


**The feet and legs' natural weapons are:**

- *Ball of the foot (Koshi)* with the toes turned upward to the maximum extent possible where tension is kept in the joints and the ankle, while the foot is in a plantar flexion (See natural weapons of Karate section).
- *Sword foot (Sokuto)* is the outer edge of the foot, which is used for attack.
- *Heel (Kakato)*
- *Instep (Haisoku)*
- *Toe tips (Tsumasaki)*
- *Knee (Hiza)*

Generally, every kick can be delivered to the four target areas: The upper level (Jodan) is the head and the neck; the middle level (Chudan) is from the base of the neck to the line going until the navel; the lower level (Gedan) is from the navel to the knees; the level below the knees (Hiza Shita).

Basically, every kick is delivered from the hips, by hip progression (especially for thrust front kick), or by hip rotation, or a combination of both, followed by the kicking leg towards the target.

There are three basic forms of execution in kicking techniques (forms regarding of hip movements):

a)  Straight kicks (hip progression): b)  Circular kicks (hip rotation + progression), or only hip progression; c)  Lateral or side kicks (abduction - adduction).

# Kicking Techniques (Keri Waza) Classification

| Name of Techniques | Hip Movements | Leg Movement Towards the Target |
|---|---|---|
| **I. Straight kicks** (Basic kick execution) | | |
| **– Front kicks** | | |
| Mae Geri Keage | Flexion (12) - Extension (13) | Straight rectilinear |
| Mae Geri Kekomi | (Progression) | movement |
| Kin Geri (kick to groin) | " | " |
| Mae Fumi Komi | " | " |
| Mae Hiza Geri | " | " |
| **– Back kicks** | | |
| Ushiro Geri | Flexion - Extension | Straight rectilinear |
| Ushiro Fumi Komi | Flexion | movement |
| **– Side kicks** | | |
| Yoko Geri Keage | Abduction - Adduction | Straight lateral |
| Yoko Geri Kekomi | " | movement |
| Yoko Fumi Komi | " | " |
| Yoko Fumi Kiri | " | " |
| **II. Circular kicks** (Basic kick execution) | | |
| O (Ko) Mawashi Geri | Rotation + Progression | Circular movement |
| Gyaku Mawashi Geri | Progression + Rotation | " |
| Mawashi Miza Geri | Rotation + Progression | " |
| Mikazuki Geri | Flexion - Extension | " |
| Gyaku Mikazuki Geri | Flexion - Extension | " |
| Ushiro Mawashi Geri | Rotation | " |
| Ushiro Gyaku Mikazuki Geri | Rotation | " |
| Ura Mawashi Geri | Progression + Rotation | " |

| Name of Techniques | Hip Movements | Leg Movement Towards the Target |
|---|---|---|
| **I. Straight kicks** **(Jumping kick execution)** | | |
| **– Front kicks** | | |
| Mae Tobi Geri | Flexion - Extension | Straight movement |
| Mae Tobi Hiza Geri | " | " |
| Nidan Geri | " | " |
| **– Side kicks** | | |
| Yoko Tobi Geri | Abduction - Adduction | Straight lateral movement |
| **II. Circular kicks** **(Jumping kick execution)** | | |
| Mawashi Tobi Geri | Rotation + Progression | Circular movement |
| Mawashi Hiza Tobi Geri | " | " |
| Ushiro Mawashi Tobi Geri | Rotation | " |
| Ushrio Gyaku Mikazuki Tobi Geri | " | " |

## Description of kicking techniques
(Figs. 64 to 71 & Photos 1 to 6)
(The major techniques)


**Front Snap Kick (Mae Geri Keage)** (Fig. 64)

This kick can be utilized from either a moving or a stationary position, with the front leg as well as the rear leg.  It also can be performed from a variety of different stances.  The area used for a front kick is the ball of the foot or instep (in groin kick).  This snap kick acquires its power from the snapping action of the lower leg aided by the hip progression movement.

Let's assume a Hidari Zenkutsu Dachi and make the attacking leg the right leg. The kicking leg's knee is raised in front of the center of the body, then the leg is straightened, hips are applied a little bit and instep straightened with toes curled back.  The leg is snapped back assuming the first position and then the hip returned to it's original position.  The upper body should be kept straight and balance maintained.


**Front Thrust Kick (Mae Geri Kekomi)** (Fig. 65 & Photo 1)

In this kick the ball of the foot, or heel, is used.  The knee is raised higher (than in Mae Geri Keage) to the chest level, then the leg is straightened forcefully from that position. Effectiveness comes from keeping the lower part of the lumbar vertebrae facing forward and

**Side Snap Kick (Yoko Geri Keage)** (Fig. 66 & Photo 2)

This kick is performed from the side of the body.  It can be practiced from Zenkutsu, Neko Ashi, Tsuru Ashi Dachi etc.  The kicking leg's knee is first raised to the side (the sole of the kicking foot could touch easily the inside part of the supporting leg's knee), then the leg is straightened.  At this time the hip raises up to augment the snapping action, with the upper body leaned easily laterally and backward, followed by the snapping of the leg back and the hip lowered, resuming the stance.

The kicking surface is the outside edge of the foot (Sokuto), including a very small part of the instep.

Fig. 64

Fig. 65                    Fig. 66

**Side Thrust Kick (Yoko Geri Kekomi)** (Fig. 67 & Photo 3)

This kick utilizes the thrusting force of the leg, which is increased by the hip.  It is more a "total pledgement" technique and requires good control of balance, keeping the recovery factor in mind.  The kicking surface is Sokuto against the face, midsection, side of the body, or lower level against the knee.  An important point to be kept in mind is that the pivoting action is on the ball of the supporting foot as the thrusting takes place.
It is important that the path of the foot in both kicking and withdrawing be the same.


**Roundhouse Kick (Mawashi Geri)** (Fig. 68 & Photo 4)

This kick is a circular snap kick using the ball of the foot (Koshi), or instep (Haisoku), as the kicking surface.  First raise the leg with the knee as high as possible in an arc from outside inward.  The calf is very close to the thigh.  The path of the leg should be nearly parallel with the floor, the hips must be rotated strongly and swiftly at the time of hitting the target and the calf must be straighten from the thigh using the snapping of the knee.  The the leg snaps back together with the hips rotating backward to its original position.

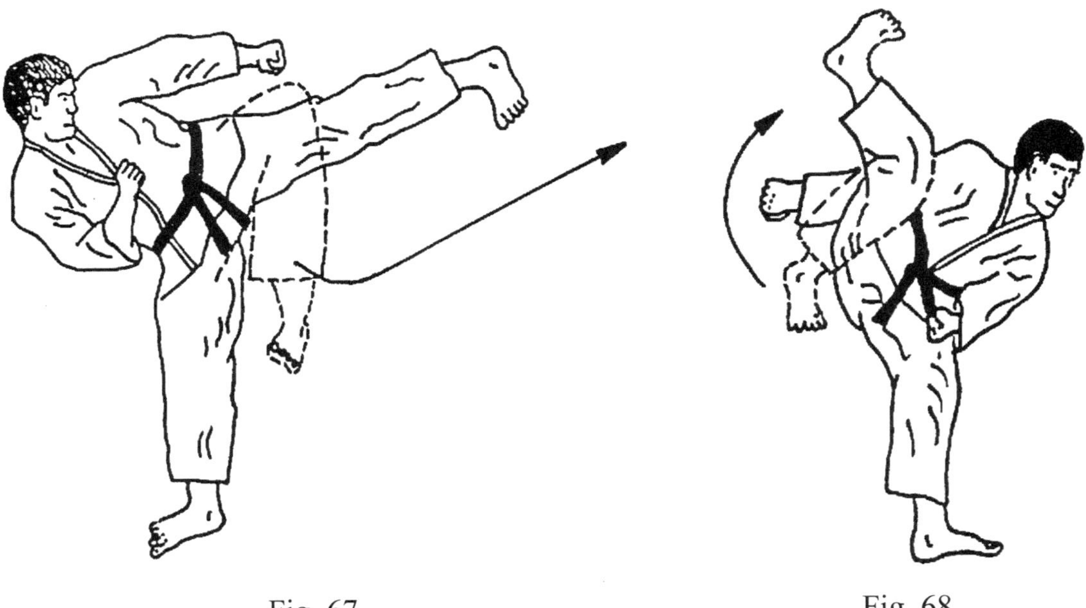

Fig. 67           Fig. 68

### Back Thrust Kick (Ushiro Geri Kekomi) (Fig. 69 & Photo 5)

This type of kick uses the thrusting action of the leg and the hip in a backwards direction, using the heel as the kicking surface. With Ushiro Geri a person can kick further than with Mae Geri. From a Shizentai position with your back towards the opponent, assuming the kicking leg will be the right one, the kicking action starts with lifting up the kicking thigh parallel with the floor and at the same time inclining the upper body in front approximately 45 degrees angle, turning the head to the right, looking at the target.

The actual kick starts now with a thrusting motion of the right leg towards the target and, at the same time, the upper body is leaning more foreward. On impact the body and the kicking leg must be on the same level and parallel with the floor. Both the hip and the kicking leg should be withdrawn back simultaneously, as in Mae Geri. The supporting leg must be well planted on the floor to maintain a good balance.

### Back Roundhouse Kick (Ushiro Mawashi Geri) (Fig. 70 & Photo 6)

This kick uses the heel, or the sole, as the kicking surface. This type of kick is a very powerful one.

From a Hidari Shizentai position, bring the kicking leg (right leg) up to the chest and turn 180 degrees angle, rotating the hips and entire body to enable the heel to make contact with the back of the neck, or face, of the opponent. On contact with the opponent's body the upper body is leaned backwards.

### Crescent Kick (Mikazuki Geri) (Fig. 72)

This type of kick can be used for an attack, or for a block, using the sole of the foot as the kicking surface. This kick is executed circularly, with a snapping motion from the knee, unless it is used as a blocking kick in which case snapping motion is used less.

Note: Fig. 72 can be seen at **5.2. Leg Blocking Techniques (Ashi Uke Waza)**, the following chapter.

*Observations: (See Fig. 71)*

1. The supporting leg has a role as a balance stabilizer and shock absorber when the sole of the foot is planted on the ground during target kicking. During free fighting (high kick executions), the heel is lifted up from the floor and the instep muscles are extended (musculi pedis flexor digitorum longus).

**a**. The sole of the foot is planted on the floor:
- – good balance
- – good possibility for absorbing shock

**b**. The sole of the foot is not planted on the floor:
- – less body balance (instability)
- – less possibility for absorbing shock
- – excellent dynamism
- – excellent manoeuvring possibilities for combination techniques

2. Arms are usually placed around the hips for maintaining the directed power in the kicking leg but, many times, they can move away from the hip region for added help in maintaining the balance.
3. Positions and stances, as many as they are, can be used for almost any kind of kicking techniques.
4. The legs and the feet are used not only for kicking but also for blocking attacks and they are classified as leg blocking techniques called Ashi Uke Waza.

Fig. 69

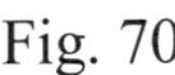

Fig. 70

Fig. 71

Photo 1

Photo 2

Photo 3

Photo 4

Photo 5

Photo 6

# *5.2.  LEG BLOCKING TECHNIQUES*
## *(Ashi Uke Waza)*
(Figs. 72, 73 & Photos 1, 2)


These leg techniques are only illustrated by Figures and Photos.  Please also see Classification of Blocking Techniques.

Fig. 72 and Photo 1 - Crescent Kick Block (Mikazuki Geri Uke), see explanation on Crescent Kick.

Fig. 73 Inside Snapping Block (Nami Ashi or Nami Gaeshi), a blocking technique in which the foot is used to deflect leg attacks to the groin or lower level.

Photo 2 - Knee Block (Hiza Uke)

Fig. 72

Fig. 73

Photo 1

Photo 2

# 6.  *THROWING TECHNIQUES*
## *(Nage Waza)*
(Figs. 74, 75 & 76)

Throwing techniques are part of *take down (Taoshi Waza)* techniques and are very important in Sendo-Ryu Karatedo.  In modern Karate sport competition, nobody scores a point for throwing or sweeping the opponent.  Points are given just for punching (striking), or kicking techniques.

In Sendo-Ryu Karatedo, takedown techniques have a special attention, due to the fact that this style is strongly oriented towards self-defense, not just on sport Karate.  For any take down action, the contestant gets 2 points, and for a punch or kick actions, the contestant gets one point.

Takedown techniques in Karate basically take in the form of legsweeping techniques (Ashi Barai) against the opponent's leg(s).  The opponent can be taken down by attacking the leg(s) with arms or legs.  After an Ashi Barai, a punch or kick should follow the action.

In Judo, contestants hold each other's Judo outfit (Judogi) and, before attempting a throwing, they execute offbalancing maneuveurs (Kuzushi).  Kuzushi is done by pulling or pushing the opponent, by holding the Judogi at the collar, sleeve, belt level, and making the opponent lose his balance by being only on the heel(s), ball of the foot, edge of the foot, or just on one leg.

From such an unbalanced - unstable position (center of gravity is outside of the body), the attacker can throw the opponent relatively easily with arm throwing techniques (Te Nage Waza); using mostly the arms in throwing action, with hip throwing techniques (Koshi Nage Waza); using mostly the hips in throwing action, with leg throwing techniques (Ashi Nage Waza) using mostly the legs in throwing action.

Leg throwing techniques from Judo are similar to Ashi Barai leg sweeping techniques in Karate.  Two major differences divide the Karate leg sweeping techniques from Judo leg throwing techniques:

In Karate, the holding of the opponent is allowed for up to two seconds and, as a result, emphasizing more on leg for sweeping, as opposed to Judo, where sweeping techniques are performed equally by the legs as well as the arms.  Because of this, Karate sweepings are primarily sweeps, while the Judo sweepings also include throwings where the opponent's body can rotate in the air approximately for a total of 270 degrees angle or less (if the opponent could make a front flip lending on its feet, that would be a 360 degrees angle flip).  This kind of a situation can happen in a "Leg Wheel" (O Guruma) or "Knee Wheel" (Hiza Guruma), technique where the Tori throws the Uke making him spin 270 degrees angle in the air. (See Fig. 74).

Only illustrated are arm throwing techniques (Te Nage Waza) and hip throwing techniques (Koshi Nage Waza).

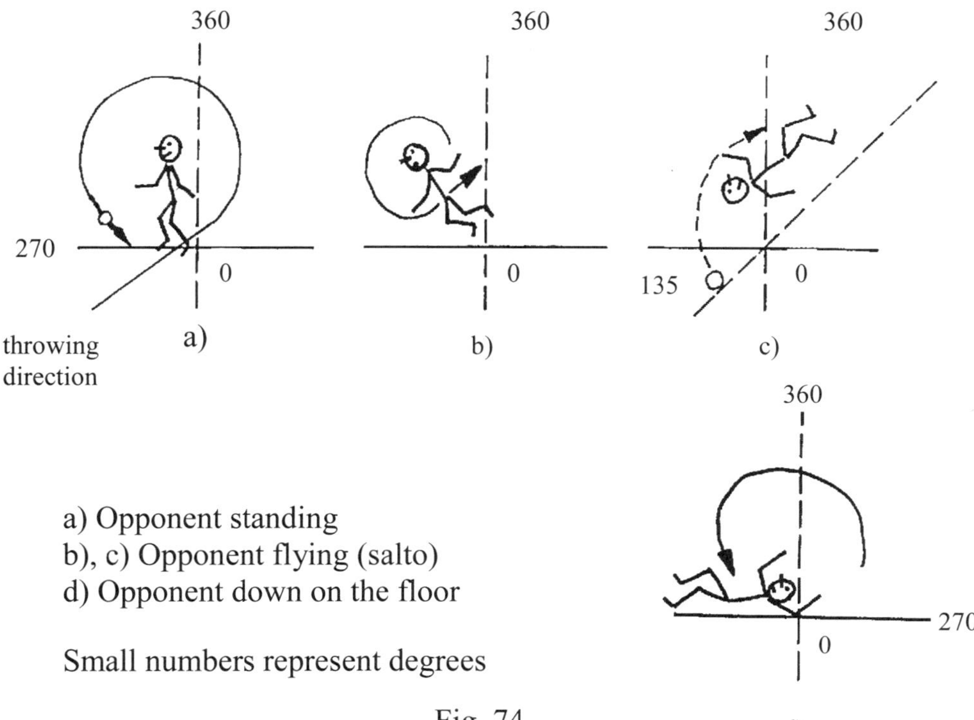



a) Opponent standing
b), c) Opponent flying (salto)
d) Opponent down on the floor

Small numbers represent degrees

Fig. 74

Te Nage Waza - Floating Throw (Uki Otoshi)

Off balancing (Kuzushi) and
preparation (Tsukuri)

Execution (Kake)

Fig. 75

Koshi Nage Waza - Changing Hip Throw (Utsuri Goshi)

Preparation (Tsukuri)          Execution (Kake)

Fig. 76

# 6.1.  *LEG SWEEPING TECHNIQUES*
## *(Ashi Barai Waza)*
(See Photos 1 to 8)

Sweeping techniques can be done in varied manners.  Sweeping techniques are executed against the lower part of the opponent's leg(s) lower half of the calf, and the executor can use the instep, or sole, as the sweeping surface.

The sweeping direction against an opponent can be:
- Forward  - Side  - Diagonal forward  - Diagonal backward.

## Sweeping techniques classification:

1) **Using front leg, or rear leg, for sweeping**
2) **Attacking the front leg, or rear leg, for sweeping**
3) **Sweeping used in attack, or in defense (tempo or stationary sweeping)**
4) **Feint sweeping, used for combination.**

**1)   Using the front leg** for sweeping can make the action faster, but less efficient, because there is less power.  **Using the rear leg**, one can make the action more powerfull because of shifting and the longer distance that the rear leg has over the front leg.

In a sweeping action, the body's height should be kept not too high, but not too deep, and the knee of the supporting leg must be bent, whereas the foot of the same leg must be planted firmly on the ground.

Sweeping actions are not kicking actions, but many people, instead of sweeping, kick the lower leg, which results in injuries and penalties in competitions.  When the sweeping leg starts its action, it should start by sweeping the ground, keeping the foot at all times on the floor.  As the sweeping leg is closing near the opponent's leg, approximately one foot away, a little bit of hitting should be emphasized on to the sweeping action.

**2)  Attacking the front leg** (Photos 1, 2) is the most used sweeping action because the opponent's front leg is closer to you and, for that reason, you can more easily sweep that leg. To sweep the front leg is not an easy task, because it can be easily withdrawn.  However, for an opponent who tends to lean forward and put his weight on his front leg, the sweeping technique will be more effective.  The sweeping direction can be any of those which have been mentioned earlier in this book.

In order to ease and make any sweeping technique more efficient (except of those feint sweeping) the opponent's arm or shoulder (sleeve, collar etc.) should be held and pulled in a certain direction.

For example, the oponent is in a left front stance (Hidari Zenkutsu Dachi); you are in a right fighting stance (Migi Mae Seishan Dachi).  At approximately the same time, with the sweeping action, you should catch the upper part (left) of the sleeve of your opponent, sweeping him to your left, then pulling him down with your right arm, and then the pulling down action will turn into a twisting motion, ending with the opponent on your left side down.

In Sendo-Ryu Karatedo you can hold and pull the opponent for three seconds and on the 4th second the opponent should be already down.


**Attacking the rear leg** (Photos 3, 4, 5) is very difficult and it is nearly impossible when your opponent has planted firmly his feet on the ground and his center of gravity is perfectly centered in the midsection of his body.

Attacking the rear leg requires timing from both Tori and Uke and, basically, the opponent must be in an offbalanced position, particularly with his weight more on his rear leg. You must force your opponent in lifting up his front leg a little, and for this you can make feints against his face, or by pushing his shoulder which can make him lean backwards, lifting up his front leg a little bit and making his rear leg main supporter of his weight.


**3)  Sweeping used in attacks** are not as effective as those used in defense.  Sweeping in attack demands more power and body shifting, therefore, more energy will be spent and more time will be needed for execution.


**Sweeping in defense** (Photos 6, 7, 8) should be done exactly in the same manner as it is done in blocking (sweeping) with the arm.

The Uke must time his sweep with the opponent's actions.  For instance, when your opponent attacks with a Migi Jun Zuki and you are in a Migi position, you must sweep the opponent's leg before it lands down.  This sweep presupposes an earlier contact with the opponent's leg and the contact of sweeping continues until the opponent is down.


**4)  Feint sweeping** can be just a very short action, usually the opponent loses his balance, then continuing with the combination action.  Feint sweeping can also be done without touching the opponent's leg, but being close enough to distract his attention and for you to continue with a punch, or kick.

Photo 1

Photo 2

Photo 3

Photo 4

Photo 5

Photo 6

Photo 7

Photo 8

# 7.  COMBINATION  TECHNIQUES
## (Renraku Waza)
(See Figs. 77a & 77b)

There is a saying in Japanese "Ikken Hisatsu" - stop the opponent with one blow, or knock down the opponent with one blow.

In the earlier years before 1970 - 1975 Karate matches lasted two minutes and went for one full point (Ippon), or two half points (Wazaari).  This meant that the combatants tried to obtain one Ippon which could be considered Ikken Hisatsu.  For this reason, Karateka all over the world trained for hard and fast attacks, which could be considered a fatal attack in real combat situations.  Because of this, the Karate matches were short in time and almost never reached two minutes and, for this reason, Karate matches lost their attraction.

Since the World Union of Karatedo Organization (WUKO)**, which is the leading body for amateur Karate Federations, was founded in 1970, the matches went from one Ippon to three Ippon (Sanbon), and Karate matches regained their attraction.  Matches became longer and contestants started using more combinations (follow up techniques).


***Combination techniques are used:***


a)  If the first attack missed, then the second or third attack would reach the target.

b)  In basic Kihon training, combinations help the Karateka develop specific endurance.

c)  Combinations also help the dynamism of the Karate techniques.

d)  Combinations are one of the important tools used for tactics.

**Presently the leading body for amateur Karate organizations is the World Karate Federation (WKF).

*Exemple of combinations:*

**A** - attacks Migi Mae Geri          **B** - defends Hidari Gedan Uke

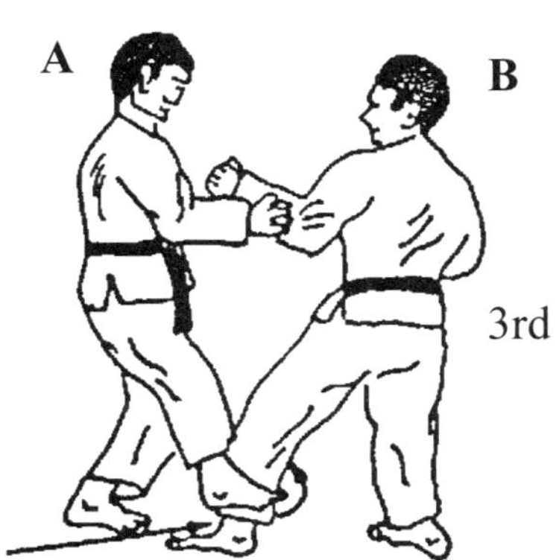 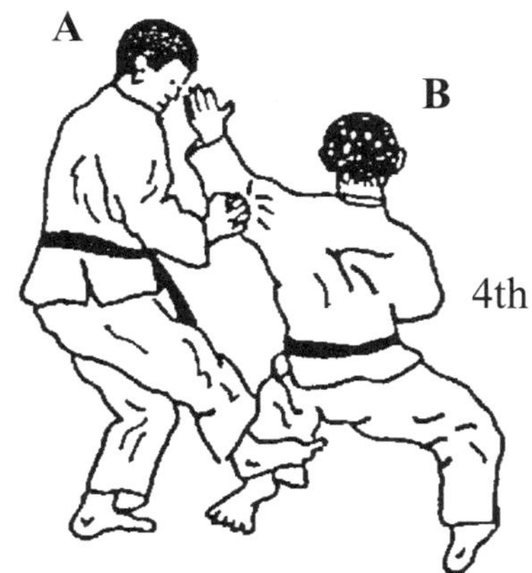

**A** - continues Migi Ashi Barai          **A** - sweeps more energically the **B**'s

**A** - continues with a left punch, while **B** is down on the ground

Fig. 77a

*Example of combinations:*

**A** - attacks Migi Mae Geri

**B** - defends Hidari Gedan Uke

**A** - continues Hidari Teisho Uchi
to **B**'s face

**A** - continues again Hidari
Mawashi Geri to **B**'s face

Fig. 77b

# 8.  *SPARRING (Kumite)*

Kumite is a type (method) of practicing karate with one, or several partners.  It is an exchange of offensive, defensive and contra offensive techniques, applied with tactics (when the Kumite is free).

If Kihon is the vehicle, or tool, of Karate, and Kata is the rigid-hard (attack-defense) meaning of Karate, then Kumite is the soft meaning of Karate, even if the attacks and defenses are executed hard, since the softness of the motions are there.

In a prearranged form of Kumite, the motions and positions are executed and kept more rigidly, like in Kata, in order to learn the correct techniques and positions, and are not changed so smoothly like in free (Jiyu Kumite) fighting.  In Kumite the Karateka learns distancing (Ma Ai), rhythm (Ri Ai), balance and how to use physical factors, such as speed, strength, endurance and skill.  They also learn how to use psychological factors, like emotions, feelings of pain and self control.

There is no separation in Karate practice between Kihon, Kata and Kumite, but Kumite can give one the necessary edge for becoming a real Karateka.

Kumite, especially Jiyu Kumite, gives practicioners the best confidence for self-protection.  Through Jiyu Kumite, the student learns how to be more tough in a real confrontation, when not all the attacks can be blocked, and where somebody can do damage to your body.

## Classification of Kumite

*There are many forms of sparring.  Kumite can be divided into four categories:*

### 1.  Basic (Kihon Kumite)

The main purpose of Kihon Kumite is to teach the student distancing between him and the opponent by practicing with a partner attacks, blocks, evading, sweeping, grabbing etc.

**a.  Sanbon Kumite** - *three steps sparring - three attacks sparring.*  It teaches the student distancing - Ma Ai, attacking, blocking and counterattacking at the same time.

**b.  Nihon Kumite** - *two steps sparring, - two attacks sparring.*  Teaches rhythm - Ri Ai, timing, using stopping attacks, such as *Sen No Sen* (high initiative in attack).

**c.  Ippon Kumite -** *one step sparring, one attack sparring.*  This fighting method is very different from other Karate styles.  This is a basic method for learning self-defense.  The student learns self-defense techniques such as blocking, throwing, sweeping, grabbing the opponent's arm, or leg, etc.  The combatant's positions are naturally high and relaxed.

In Ippon Kumite, the defense is based on the attacker's principle of ***"Ikken Hisatsu"*** (to kill or kock down with one blow).  This means that, for a first attack, there must be a definitive block and counter attack *excluding any possibility* that allows the attacker to continue his first attack with follow up techniques.  Based on this theory, the defender should throw, or sweep, his attacker because any off-balancing techniques minimize the attacker's chance to continue his attack.

### 2.  Basic formal sparring (Kihon Kata Kumite)

This type of Kumite is prearranged and is mandatory in Sendo-Ryu Karatedo.  This form of sparring is practiced with one to three steps, with three to five attacks, blocks and counterattacks.  This method is where the evasions (Kawashi) and sweeping blocks (Nagashi Uke) are emphasized.

### 3.  Prearranged sparring (Yaku Soku Kumite)

This type of sparring is the most advanced as well as the most important type of sparring, which is used before free sparring (Jiyu Kumite).  In Yaku Soku Kumite, the instructor can establish any type of technique that can be used, and possibilities of countering or escaping.  Once, however, the technique has been prearranged, no other possibilities may be used.  This type of method develops strong self-control.

*a. Yaku Soku Nihon Kumite* - prearranged two attacks sparring.  In this type of Kumite, the Tori must use two attacks (prearranged), which can be either arm technique, leg technique, or both.  Stopping attacks are not allowed.

### 4.  Free sparring (Jiyu Kumite)

**a.**  One against one, or  **b.**  One against more assailants.  Any kind of attacks, blocks, counterattacks , multiple attacks and sweeps are allowed, but they must be executed relatively soft.  The meaning of soft is about letting your mind work freely.

Jiyu Kumite is not allowed to be practiced by beginners, but only after 8-10 months practice.  The Kihon and Kata practices are needed to take place for Jiyu Kumite.

In Sendo-Ryu Karatedo, the punches and kicks are fully executed into the opponent's body.  At the Chudan level, the combatants must hit as hard as they can to the stomach, chest, ribs.  At the face level, the attacks must be executed with a touching of the opponent's face rather then a fully executed attack.

This full contact conception to the stomach and easy contact to the face is valid just for the advanced level Karateka (black belt and some brown belts).

# 8.1.  THREE STEPS SPARRING
## (Sanbon Kumite)
(Sanbon Kumite Photos 1 to 50)

The Uke is in Shizentai position in any Sanbon Kumite exercise, and the Tori is in Hidari Hanmi Gamae when attacking with the leg, or in Hidari Zenkutsu Dachi, when attacking with the arm.

### 1.  *IPPONME (Go No Sen)* - Tsuki to Chudan (Photos 1 to 7)

Preparation position (Photo 1).  Tori will attack with a Migi Jun Zuki to the Chudan, while Uke moves back into Migi Mae Seishan Dachi, blocking the attack with a Migi Chudan Uchi Uke (Photo 2).  Tori will attack again with a Hidari Chudan Jun Zuki.  Uke will move back into a Hidari Mae Seishan Dachi, blocking the attack with Hidari Chudan Uchi Uke (Photo 3).  Tori attacks with a Migi Chudan Jun Zuki, while Uke moves back into a half step with his left leg (behind his right leg) (Photo 4), after this action Uke's right leg moves forward to his right into Migi Mae Seishan Dachi or Migi Fudo Dachi and, at the same time, with his changed position, his left arm blocks Tori's attack with Hidari Gedan Uke (Photo 5), and counters with his right fist with Migi Age Ura Zuki to Tori's chin (Photo 6, 7).

Photo 1

Photo 2

Photo 3

Photo 4

Photo 5

Photo 6

Photo 7

### 2. *NIHONME (Go No Sen)* - **Tsuki to Jodan and Geri** (Photos 8 to 13)

Preparation position (Photo 8).  Tori attacks with a Migi Jodan Jun Zuki.  Uke moves back into Migi Mae Seishan Dachi, blocking the attack with Migi Jodan Uchi Uke, or Migi Age Uke (Photo 9).  Tori continues his attack with a Hidari Jodan Jun Zuki, Uke moves back into a left position, blocking the attack with Hidari Jodan Uchi Uke, (Photo 10), then Tori attacks with Migi Mae Geri (Photo 11).  Tori follows with Migi Jodan Jun Zuki attack.  Uke holds the previous position sliding back and sidewards to his right, blocking first Tori's Mae Geri with a Hidari Gedan Uke, (Photo 11) then blocking Tori's Jun Zuki with a Hidari Jodan Soto Uke (Photo 12) and, at the same time, punching Tori's face with Hidari Mae Te Zuki (Photo 13).

Photo 8

Photo 9

Photo 10

Photo 11

Photo 12

Photo 13

Soke Arus on right, poses with the legendary
Budoka, O-Sensei Philip S. Porter - President of
the USMartial Arts Association at the banquet of
USMA Hall of Fame August 12, 2000.
Prof. Arus has been inducted in Hall of Fame
2000 Millennium

Prof. Arus poses with Okinawan
Supreme master Fusei Kise 10th Dan
after a training session at USMA -
Hall of Fame August 12, 2000.
Supreme master Fusei Kise backed up
Prof. Emeric Arus for Sendo-Ryu

### 3. *SANBONME (Sen No Sen)* - **Geri to Chudan** (Photos 14, 15, 16)

Uke is in Shizentai, Tori is in left fighting position (Hidari Hanmi Gamae).  Tori attacks with a Migi Mae Geri, Uke moves back into Migi Hanmi Gamae, avoiding Tori's kick (Photo 14).  Tori attacks again with Hidari Chudan Mae Geri, Uke moves back into Hidari Hanmi Gamae, avoiding Tori's kick (Photo 15).  Tori attacks for the third time, again with right leg front kick.  Uke remains in his left position, sliding easily backward diagonally and to the right, stopping Tori's attack with a Hidari Yoko Geri Keage Kekomi to Tori's stomach (Photo 16).

Photo 14

Photo 15

Photo 16

### *4. YONHONME (Go No Sen)* **- Geri to Chudan** (Photos 17, 18, 19)

The starting position is the same as in # 3. SANBONME, and the attacks and defenses, are also the same as previously in the first and second step.  When Tori attacks for the third time with Migi Mae Geri, Uke from his left position moves with his left foot backward with a half step just behind his right leg and , at the same time, blocking Tori's kick with Migi Gedan Uchi Haiwan Barai (Photo 17), with his right foot Uke steps forward and to the right with a half step, thus being in a Migi Hanmi Gamae position and stopping Tori's action with a Migi Mae Empi Uchi to Tori's chin (Photo 18 & 19).

Photo 17                          Photo 18

Photo 19

### 5.  *GOHONME (Go No Sen)* - **Tsuki to Chudan** (Photos 20 to 24)

The starting position is the same as in # 1. IPPONME.  Tori attacks three times with a Migi, Hidari and Migi Jodan Jun Zuki.  Uke defends three times with Migi, Hidari and Migi Jodan Haito Uke (Photos 20, 21, 22).  Uke holds right fighting position or Kokutsu Dachi position, (Photo 23) at the third Haito Uke, without waisting time, Uke grabs Tori's wrist pulling him forward and countering, at the same time, with a Hidari Gyaku Zuki to Tori's ribs (Photo 24).

Photo 20　　　　　Photo 21

Photo 22　　　　　Photo 23

Photo 24

### 6.  *ROPPONME (Go No Sen)* - **Tsuki to Chudan** (Photos 25, 26, 27)

The starting position is the same as in # 1. IPPONME.  Tori attacks three times with a Migi, Hidari and Migi Chudan Jun Zuki.  Uke defends three times with Migi, Hidari and Migi Chudan Soto Uke (Photos 25, 26).  The first two blocks, Migi and Hidari are executed in Mae Seishan Dachi, and the third block is executed in Migi Fudo Dachi.  Uke steps a little bit more outside to the left with his left leg, then with the right arm, in a blocking action, grabs Tori's right wrist, pulling him towards his right side and then countering with a Hidari Jodan Gyaku Zuki (Photo 27).  Uke now turns into Migi Zenkutsu Dachi.

Photo 25

Photo 26

### 7.  *SHICHIHONME (Go No Sen)*
**Tsuki to Chudan** (Photos 28 to 32)

Photo 27

The starting position is the same as in # 1. IPPONME.  Tori attacks three times with Migi, Hidari and Migi Chudan Jun Zuki.  Uke will defend three times Migi, Hidari and Migi Chudan Uchi Uke (Photos 28, 29).  At Tori's last attack, Uke blocks with his right arm and, at the same time, catches Tori's right wrist with the left hand.  Uke now holds Tori's arm, executing a Migi Shuto Uchi to Tori's neck, (Photo 30) and immediately pushing Tori's right shoulder with his right palm (Photo 31) and executes a Minor Inside Reap technique (Migi Ko Uchi Gari) (Photo 32).

Photo 28

Photo 29

Photo 30

Photo 31

Photo 32

## 8.  *HACHIHONME (Go No Sen)* - **Tsuki to Chudan and Jodan** (Photos 33, 34)

The starting position is the same as in # 1. IPPONME.  Tori attacks three times with Migi *Chudan* Jun Zuki, Hidari *Chudan* Jun Zuki and Migi *Jodan* Jun Zuki.  Uke blocks the first attack with Migi Chudan Uchi Uke, the second attack with Hidari Chudan Uchi Uke and now he is in a left position.  When Tori attacks to the face, Uke moves his left leg a little bit behind his own right leg and, at the same time, shifts his right leg forward, blocking Tori's attack with Hidari Jodan Soto Uke (Photo 33) countering Tori's chin with a Migi Tate Zuki (Photo 34).

Note:  The Tai Sabaki for the third block is executed just like in # 1. IPPONME.

Photo 33

Photo 34

### 9.  KYUHONME (Go No Sen) - Tsuki to Jodan (Photos 35 to 40)

The staring position is the same as in # 1. IPPONME.  Tori attacks three times with Migi, Hidari and Migi Jodan Jun Zuki.  Uke blocks with Migi then Hidari Jodan Age Uke and the third block with Migi Jodan Shuto Age Uke (Photos 35, 36, 37).  Tori is now in Migi Mae Seishan Dachi.  After the block, Uke catches and pulls down Tori's right arm and executes a Hidari Mawashi Empi Uchi to Tori's cheek (Photo 38), then Uke's left palm slides down on Tori's right forearm, pressing or hitting it with Ox Jaw Hand (Seiryuto) (Photo 39), then executing a Migi Jodan Ura Zuki or Migi Jodan Teisho Uchi to Tori's face (Photo 40).

Photo 35

Photo 36

Photo 37

Photo 38

Photo 39

Photo 40

### 10. *JUPPONME (Sen)* - **Tsuki to Jodan** (Photos 41 to 47)

Preparation position (Photo 41).  Tori attacks three times with Migi, Hidari and Migi Jodan Jun Zuki.  Uke blocks with Migi and Hidari Jodan Age Uke both times in Zenkutsu Dachi (Photos 42, 43).  When Tori attacks the third time with the right arm to Jodan, Uke, still holding his left arm, slides backward diagonally to the right from Hidari Zenkutsu Dachi to Hidari Han Mae Seishan Dachi (Photo 44), now Uke preparing his left foot's inside part of the sole (Photo 45), sweeps Tori's right ankle from behind (Photos 46, 47).

The sweeping is similar to that of Judo's, Major Inside Reap (O Uchi Gari) technique, but the attacks is made with the sole and not with the calf.  The left sweeping foot works with a semicircular motion from right to the left and back.  Uke should not block the attack and Uke's body should be inclined backward to his right.

Photo 41

Photo 42

Photo 43

Photo 44     Photo 45     Photo 46     Photo 47

### 11. *JUIPPONME (Go No Sen)* - **Geri attack** (Photos 48, 49, 50)

The starting position is the same as in # 3. SANBONME.  Tori attacks three times with Migi, Hidari and Migi Mae Geri.  Uke defends the first kick moving back into Migi Mae Seishan Dachi and, at the same time, with his right forearm defends against Tori's right kick. (The technique used for defense is Gedan Uchi Haiwan Barai) (Photo 48).  Tori continues his attack with a left kick, Uke defends by moving back into Hidari Mae Seishan Dachi (Photo 49). Tori now executes the third kick (right leg kick).  Uke holds the left position, but his right leg moves to the right into Hidari Fudo Dachi and, at the same time, Uke's left forearm blocks the kick and he is countering with Tate Gyaku Zuki to the face or stomach (Photo 50).

Photo 48     Photo 49     Photo 50

# 8.2.  *TWO STEPS SPARRING*
## *(Nihon Kumite)*
(Nihon Kumite Photos 1 to 48)

### *1. IPPONME (Sen No Sen)* - **Tsuki** (Photos 1 to 4)

Tori and Uke are in right figthing stance (Photo 1).  Tori attacks with migi Jodan Tobi Komi Zuki.  Uke slides backward holding the right position and defending against Tori's punch with Migi Teisho Nagashi Uke (Photo 2).  Uke must slide back sufficiently in order to keep Tori pretty far, otherwise Tori can follow up with a reverse punch, or any other attack.  Tori makes the second attack a Hidari Jodan Jun Zuki (Photo 3).  Uke slides forward just half the distance that he did (backward) before and executes a blocking punch Migi Jodan Uke Zuki (Photo 4).

Photo 1

Photo 2

Photo 3

Photo 4

**Variation for IPPONME**

The same exercise as the previous one, but Uke, instead of executing Migi Jodan Uke Zuki, will block  with Migi Jodan Soto Uke and counter at the same time with Hidari Gyaku Zuki.

*Note:  For returning into Shizentai position in all Nihon Kumite please see 4. YONHONME.*

### 2. NIHONME (Sen No Sen) - Geri and Tsuki (Photos 5, 6, 7)

Tori and Uke are both in Migi Mae Seishan Dachi (Photo 5).  Tori attacks with a Migi Jodan Surikomi Mawashi Geri, Uke defends easily retreating and holding his right position, then executes a double arm block (Photo 6).  Tori continues his attack with Hidari Gyaku Zuki to stomach (Photo 7).  Uke executes a Migi Chudan Uke Tate Zuki *(he should not block, but rather stop Tori's attack)* (Photo 7).

| Photo 5 | Photo 6 | Photo 7 |

### 3. SANBONME (Go No Sen) - Geri and Geri (Photos 8 to 11)

Tori is in a right and Uke is in a left fighting position (Photo 8).  Tori attacks with Migi Jodan Surikomi Mawashi Geri; Uke retreats easily in the same position and blocks Tori's attack with Hidari Empi Uke (Photo 9).  Tori attacks now with Hidari Chudan Mae Geri.  Uke executes a Migi Gedan Barai (Photo 10) and executes a Tai Sabaki turning backwards to the right, his foot in a half circle rotation.  At the same time he executes a Hidari Shuto Uchi to Tori's neck (Photo 11).

Photo 8

Photo 9

Photo 10

Photo 11

### 4.  *YONHONME (Sen No Sen)* - **Tsuki and Geri** (Photos 12 to 17)

Both combatants are in right fighting position (Photo 12).  Tori attacks with Migi Jodan Tobi Komi Zuki; Uke slides backward and, blocking the attack with Migi Te Nagashi Uke (Photo 13).  Tori continues his attack with Migi Surikomi Mae Geri (Photo 14), Uke slides forward diagonally to the right and stops in Migi Fudo Dachi, blocking the kick with Hidari Gedan Barai and counters, at the same time, Tori's face with Migi Tate Zuki (Photo 14)  After the completion of attack and defense, they will return to Shizentai position (Photos 15, 16, 17).

Photo 12

Photo 13

Photo 14

Photo 15

Photo 16

Photo 17

### 5. *GOHONME (Sen No Sen)* - **Tsuki and Geri** (Photos 18, 19, 20)

Tori and Uke are both in a right fighting position (Photo 18). Tori steps forward and executes a Migi Chudan Gyaku Zuki (Photo 19). Uke steps backward and blocks with a Hidari Chudan Uchi Uke (Photo 19). Uke now is in a Hidari Mae Seishan Dachi. Tori continues his attack with Migi Jodan Mawashi Geri and, at the same time, Uke blocks and counters by inclining his body to the front, lifting up his left arm and blocking with his elbow and upper arm, then pushing his left fist into Tori's chin, Uke's right palm controls Tori's right knee (Photo 20).

Photo 18

Photo 19

Photo 20

### 6. *ROPPONME (Sen No Sen)* **-Tsuki and Tsuki** (Photos 21, 22, 23)

Tori is in a left, Uke is in a right fighting position (Photo 21).  Tori attacks with Migi Jodan Jun Zuki and Uke moves back into Hidari Mae Seishan Dachi and blocks Tori's attack with Hidari Jodan Soto Uke (Photo 22).  Tori starts to execute Hidari Jodan Jun Zuki, while Uke, by simply opening his right palm, blocks Tori's fist and at the same time stops Tori's chin with a left open palm trust - Teisho Zuki (Photo 23).

Photo 21       Photo 22       Photo 23

### 7. *SHICHIHONME (Go No Sen)* **- Tsuki and Tsuki** (Photos 24 to 28)

Tori is in a left, Uke is in a right fighting position (Photo 24).  Tori steps forward and executes a Migi Jodan Jun Zuki (Photo 25).  Uke moves back into a left position and blocks Tori's attack with Hidari Jodan Soto Ude Uke (Photo 25).  Tori now steps forward and executes a Hidari Jodan Jun Zuki (Photo 26).  Uke, at the same time, executes a Hidari Jodan Teisho Zuki and a Migi Jodan Haishu Uke (Photo 27), and Minor Inside Reap with the left leg - Hidari Ko Uchi Gari (Photo 28).

Photo 24       Photo 25

Photo 26

Photo 27

Photo 28

### 8. *HACHIHONME (Go No Sen)* - **Tsuki and Uchi** (Photo 29 to 36)

Tori is in a left, Uke is in a right position (Photo 29). Tori attacks with Migi Jodan Jun Zuki (Photo 30). Uke steps back into a left fighting position and blocks Tori's attack with Hidari Soto Ude Uke (Photo 30). Now, Tori slides forward in the same position, attacking Uke's face with a Migi Uraken Uchi (Photo 31). Uke slides back in the same position and blocks Tori's attack with a Hidari Uchi Ude Uke and, at the same time, counters Tori's chest with a Migi Tate Gyaku Zuki (Photo 32). After this completion, Uke grabs with his left palm Tori's right wrist, twisting his arm backward and to right (Tori's). Simultaneously Uke's right forearm pushes Tori's upside elbow region downward (Photo 33). Uke steps with his right leg outside of Tori's right leg, executing an easy hook against Tori's right leg (Photo 34). Finally, Tori falls down on his back (Photo 35), and at the same time, Uke pulls Tori's right arm upwards stabilizing him and punching him in the ribs (Photo 36).

Photo 29

Photo 30

Photo 31

Photo 32

Photo 33

Photo 34

Photo 35

Photo 36

### 9. *KYUHONME (Sen No Sen)* - **Gyaku Zuki and Geri** (Photo 37 to 45)

Both Tori and Uke are in a left position (Photo 37).  Tori steps forward and punches with Hidari Chudan Gyaku Zuki (Photo 38).  Uke steps back into a right position and blocks Tori's punch with Migi Chudan Uchi Uke (Photo 38).  Tori now executes a short Surikomi Migi Mae Geri (Photo 39), Uke now slides a bit in front and to the right, blocking Tori's kick with a Hidari Gedan Barai and at the same time, hitting Tori's face with a Migi Jodan Uraken Uchi (Photo 40).  Uke now turns his back to Tori and executes a Judo throw (Kubi Nage). Uke's right arm (biceps part) is under Tori's chin pushing Tori's throat (Photo 41).  Uke's left forearm surrounds Tori's neck with his thumb touching Tori's neck (Photo 42).  After the throwing completion (Photo 43 & 44), Uke finalizes with a Shita Uraken Uchi to Tori's face (Photo 45).

Photo 37

Photo 38

Photo 39

Photo 40

Photo 41

Photo 42

Photo 43

Photo 44

Photo 45

**10.  *JUHONME (Sen No Sen)* - Geri and Geri** (Photos 46, 47, 48)

Tori and Uke are in a right fighting position (Photo 46).  Tori attacks with Migi Surikomi Mae Geri; Uke slides backwards easily and blocks with Gedan Uchi Haiwan Barai (Photo 47), Tori continues his attack with a Hidari Jodan Mawashi Geri; Uke stops him with a Migi Chudan Yoko Geri (Photo 48).

Photo 46                      Photo 47                      Photo 48

# 8.3.  ONE STEP SPARRING
# (Ippon Kumite)
(Ippon Kumite Photos 1 to 41)

**1.  *IPPONME (Sen No Sen)*** (Photos 1 to 10)

Both Tori and Uke are in Migi Seishan Dachi (Photo 1).  Tori slides forward and punches Uke's face (Photo 2).  At the same time, Uke parries and, gliding simultaneously towards Tori, executes an elbow strike to Tori's face (Photo 3) and sets offbalance Tori's posture.  Uke's and Tori's right knees touch each other.  Uke lifts up his right arm (Photo 4), hitting Tori's left kidney with Haito Uchi (Photo 5), then grabbing Tori's belt (Photo 6) and pushing Tori's knee, and, at the same time, pulls Tori with the right arm towards his right with a backward motion (Photo 7), which is followed by Tori's forward fall (Photo 8).  After the fall, Tori will stand up (Photos 9, 10).

Photo 1

Photo 2

Photo 3

Photo 4

Photo 5

Photo 6

Photo 7

Photo 8

Photo 9

Photo 10

### 2. *NIHONME (Go No Sen)* (Photos 11 to 16)

Tori is in a right, Uke is in a left, position (Photo 11).  Tori slides forward and punches Uke's face; Uke parries and, at the same time, leaning back a bit, executes a left roundhouse kick outside Tori's thigh (Photo 12), then makes a follow up counter to Tori's neck, striking with Migi Haito Uchi  (Photo 13).  Now, Uke moves forward and grabs, with his right thumb, Tori's left collar and introduces his left forearm under Tori's bottom (Photo 14), and executes a Judo throwing technique, Te Guruma, arm wheel (Photo 15).  After the fall, Uke executes a downward stamping kick (Photo 16).

Photo 11

Photo 12

Photo 13

Photo 14

Photo 15

Photo 16

### 3. *SANBONME (Go No Sen)* (Photos 17 to 21)

Both Tori and Uke are in a left fighting stance (Photo 17). Tori slides forward in the same position and punches Uke's face (Photo 18). Uke retreats a little in the same position and defending Tori's attack with a Hidari Jodan Soto Uke (Photo 18). Then Uke slides forward in the same position, punching Tori's ribs with Migi Ura Zuki and, at the same time, grabs with the left palm Tori's left wrist (Photo 19). Now Uke is in a Han Zenkutsu Dachi position. He sets down his right knee setting his right palm under Tori's left knee (the palm touches Tori's inside part of the calf) (Photo 20). Uke now pushes Tori's left arm and lifts Tori's left leg throwing him with a rotative motion from down to up with his right arm and from up to down with his left arm (Photo 21).

Photo 17

Photo 18

Photo 19

Photo 20

Photo 21

### 4. *YONHONME (Sen No Sen)* (Photos 22 to 28)

Both Tori and Uke are in a left fighting position (Photo 22) (Uke can hold right position too).  Tori advances easily in the same position and executes a left straight punch, as a feint, towards Uke's face and Uke executes a left arm Jodan Soto Uke (Photo 23).  Tori pulls back his left arm and executes a Mawashi Zuki to Uke's face again with his left arm, Uke blocks with a Hidari Jodan Uchi Uke, (Photo 24) grabbing Tori's wrist with his right palm and, at the same time, stepping forward with his left leg, executing a Hidari Mae Empi Uchi (elbow strike) to Tori's face (Photo 25).  Uke now kneels down on his left knee still holding Tori's left arm (Photo 26) and executing a Judo throw similar to Uki Otoshi (Photos 27, 28).

Photo 22

Photo 23

Photo 24

Photo 25

Photo 26

Photo 27

Photo 28

### 5. *GOHONME (Go No Sen)* (Photos 29 to 35)

Tori is in a left position while Uke is in a right position.  Tori grabs Uke's right collar with his left arm (Photo 29) and punches towards Uke's face with his right fist (Photo 30).  Uke defends with his left palm, pushing Tori's fist to the right (Photos 30, 31), then Uke grabs with his right palm Tori's right wrist, leading it above Tori's left arm and also grabs with his left palm Tori's left wrist (Photo 32, 32a).  Uke turns his body a little bit to the right throwing Tori on his (Uke's) right side with an Aikido technique, cross arm throwing (Juji Nage), (Photos 33, 34).  After completing the throw, Uke can immobilize Tori's left arm (Photo 35).

Photo 29

Photo 30

Photo 31

Photo 32

Photo 32a

Photo 33

Photo 34

Photo 35

### 6. *ROPPONME (Sen No Sen)* (Photos 36 to 41)

Both Tori and Uke are in Migi position (Photo 36).  Tori slides forward and punches with Jodan Tobi Komi Zuki (Photo 37).  Uke slides forward diagonally to the right and blocks Tori's attack with his left arm (Hidari Jodan Age Uke) Uke, still in Migi position, now slides his right leg forward in Han Zenkutsu Dachi and executes a double punch (Yama Zuki) (Photo 37), Uke's left arm punches Tori's face, with his right arm punches Tori's stomach.  Uke leans forward, grabbing Tori's legs behind his thighs (Photos 38, 39) and executes a Judo throwing technique (Morote Gari) (Photo 40) and a stamping kick to the groin (Kakato Geri) (Photo 41).

***(Note:  In Sendo-Ryu Karate style there are a total of 12 Ippon Kumite requirements. Six have been described).***

Photo 36

Photo 37

Photo 38

Photo 39

Photo 40

Photo 41

# 8.4.  BASIC FORMAL SPARRING
## (Kihon Kata Kumite)
### (Photos 1 to 49)

### 1. IPPONME (Photos 1 to 10)

Both Tori and Uke are in a right fighting position (Photo 1).  Tori attacks with Migi Tobi Komi Zuki to Uke's face.  Uke easily inclines his head to the right and defends with Migi Te Nagashi Uke (Photo 2).  Tori continues his attack with Hidari Chudan Gyaku Zuki exactly to Uke's solar plexus;  Uke executes a Migi Gedan Osae Uke (Photo 3), his Naiwan of ulna bone will press Tori's forearm close to the wrist down and towards Uke's stomach (Photo 3).  Tori's left forearm is twisted and you can see his Shuwan part of the forearm having contact with Uke's Naiwan part of the ulna bone.

At the same time, with the pressing action, Uke will grab with his left palm Tori's wrist twisting it to his (Uke's) left (Photo 4).  Uke firmly holds Tori's left wrist and executes a Migi Uraken Uchi to Tori's face (Photo 5).  After the Uraken Uchi, Uke opens his right fist in a Shuto position and pushes Tori's face (Photo 6), turning him over to his left side and, at the same time, Uke executes with his right foot a sweeping technique - inside minor reap (Ko Uchi Gari) - against Tori's right foot (Photos 7, 8).  After Tori is turned over, he will land on his back (Photo 9), then he will be turned over to his stomach.  Uke now holds firmly Tori's left wrist (with two hands) which is bent (Photo 10).

Photo 1

Photo 2

Photo 3

Photo 4

Photo 5

Photo 6

Photo 7

Photo 8

Photo 9

Photo 10

## 2. *NIHONME* (Photos 11 to 22)

Both Tori and Uke are in a right fighting position (Photo 11).  Tori attacks with Migi Tobi Komi Zuki; Uke slides back easily and defends with Migi Te Nagashi Uke (Photo 12). Tori continues his attack with Hidari Chudan Gyaku Zuki exactly to Uke's right ribs (Photo 13).  Uke executes a Migi Gedan Empi Uke from the inside out.  This block must be done with Uke's lower part of his forearm (upper part of his elbow) (Photo 14).  After this block is completed, Uke's right forearm executes a half circle from the left to the right, then grabbing with his left palm Tori's left fist (Photo 15), then locking Tori's fist between his right forearm and left palm.

Now Tori's fist turns upwards, due to Uke's pressure from his left palm which is turning/twisting to Uke's left, then Uke also grabs with his right palm Tori's left fist (Photo 16).

Uke now can throw Tori to Uke's left, (Photos 17, 18).  Tori will be rolled over on his back, (Photo 19), then he will be forced on his stomach where Uke will apply pressure against Tori's wrist (Photos 20, 21, 22).

Photo 11

Photo 12

Photo 13

Photo 14

Photo 15

Photo 16

Photo 17

Photo 18

Photo 19

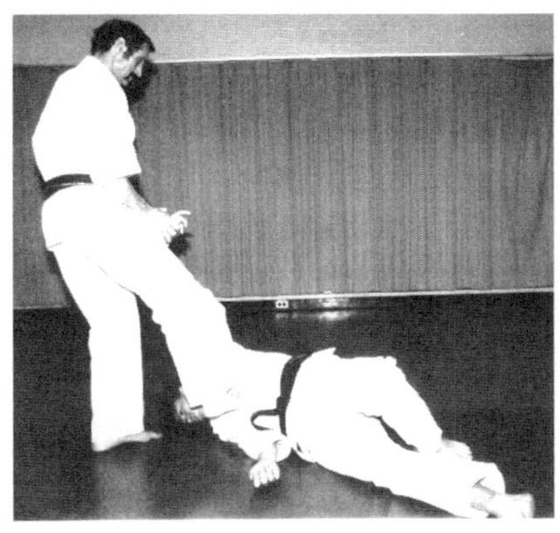

Photo 20

Photo 21

Photo 22

### 3. *SANBONME* (Photos 23 to 32)

Tori and Uke are in Migi Mae Seishan Dachi position (Photo 23).  Tori executes a Surikomi Jodan Mawashi Geri (Photos 24, 25).  Uke retreats backwards easily and blocks the kick with Ryo Ude Uke (Photo 25).  Tori slides forward easily in the same position and continues his attack with a Hidari Chudan Gyaku Zuki (Photo 26) Uke, being previously in Migi Mae Seishan Dachi, now blocks Tori's attack with Migi Gedan Osae Uke and pulls his right leg backwards into Migi Shizentai (Photo 26).  Tori now moves his right foot a little bit to his left (Photo 27) then turns 180 degrees angle to the left (Photo 28) and executes a Hidari Ushiro Geri (Photo 29) and, at the same time, Uke blocks the kick with a Hidari Sukui Uke, (left arm scooping block), and steps forward with his both legs (Photo 30).  Uke now lifts and holds Tori's left leg, at the same time stepping closer to Tori and grabbing with his right palm Tori's collar (Photo 31), then executing a right leg sweeping against Tori's right leg throwing him on the back (Photo 32), after that finalizing with a left arm punch when Tori is already on the ground.

Photo 23

Photo 24

Photo 25

Photo 26

<table>
<tr><td align="center">Photo 27</td><td align="center">Photo 28</td><td align="center">Photo 29</td></tr>
<tr><td align="center">Photo 30</td><td align="center">Photo 31</td><td align="center">Photo 32</td></tr>
</table>

### 4. YONHONME (Photos 33 to 40)

Both Tori and Uke are in Hidari Mae Seishan Dachi position (Photo 33).  Uke now *becomes an attacker*.  Uke slides forward and punches with a Tobi Komi Zuki to Tori's face (Photo 34).  Tori slides backward (both remain in left position).  Uke continues his attack with a Migi Mae Geri and Tori steps back into a right position (Photo 35).  When Uke finishes his right leg attack, both opponents remain in a right position (Photo 36).

Tori now counterattacks with a short Surikomi Migi Mae Geri to Chudan or Gedan (Photo 37).  Uke now slides quickly backwards to his left, executing a Migi Haishu Gedan Barai against Tori's kick (Photo 37).  After Uke's blocking action, he slides with both of his legs close to Tori's legs, Uke's right knee (outer margin of popliteal space) touches Tori's right leg (popliteal space) and, at the same time, grabs with his left palm Tori's right wrist and simultaneously executes a Migi Haito Uchi to Tori's left side of the neck (Photo 38).  Uke holds Tori's right wrist and pushes Tori's neck with the right forearm, throwing him above Uke's right thigh (Photo 39), and completing the throw with a right punch, or right spear hand (Nukite) (Photo 40).

Photo 33

Photo 34

Photo 35

Photo 36

Photo 37

Photo 38

Photo 39

Photo 40

## 5. *GOHONME* (Photos 41 to 49)

Both Tori and Uke are in a left position (Photo 41). Uke again *becomes an attacker.* Uke attacks with Migi Jodan Jun Zuki. Tori steps back blocking the attack with Migi Uchi Shuto Uke (Photo 42). Uke continues a Hidari Gyaku Zuki to Chudan (Tori's ribs) (Photo 43). Then, bringing forward his left leg, he sweeps Tori's right leg (Photo 44). During Uke's sweep execution, Tori moves his right leg next to his left for his balance recovery and turns his entire body to his left trying to avoid the offbalancing of his position (Photo 45). After this, Tori can execute a Hidari Ushiro Mawashi Geri to Uke's kidney (Photo 46), or can execute a Hidari Kaiten Uraken Uchi, or even an Empi Uchi to Uke's face. Uke still in a left position is easily sliding forward to his right in order to avoid Tori's kick or strike. Uke grabs with his right palm Tori's collar, pulling him back and executing with his right sole a stamping kick against Tori's right popliteal space pulling with the arm and pushing him down with the leg (Photos 47, 48).

Finally, when Tori is down, Uke executes a punch with his left fist (Photo 49).

*(Note:   In Sendo-Ryu Karate style there are a total of 12 Kihon Kata Kumite requirements, 5 have been described).*

Photo 41

Photo 42

Photo 43

Photo 44

Photo 45

Photo 46

Photo 47

Photo 48

Photo 49

# 8.5.  *KNIFE  KATA (Tanto Kata)*
(Photos 1 to 101)

### *1. IPPONME* (Photos 1 to 7)

After the salute (Rei), Tori is holding, in his left hand, the knife (Tanto) which is inside the scabbard (Saya).  Tori steps forward with his left leg, pulling the knife out from the scabbard.  Uke steps back with is right leg.  Both opponents are in a left position (Photo 1).  (In this photo the scabbard is not shown).

Tori slides forward in the same position three times and each time he raises his left fist a little bit with the scabbard as a feint.  Immediately after the third glide, he steps forward into a right position and tries to stab upwards and straight into Uke's stomach (Photo 2).  Uke retreats with his left leg into a right position and blocks the attack with Gedan Juji Uke (Photo 2); palms are open (the right palm is above the left).  The block is executed exactly against the middle part of Tori's forearm, then the two palms slide down on Tori's wrist.  Now Tori's back hand will be held and twisted to Uke's right by Uke (Photos 2a, 2b) and (Photo 3).

Uke holding Tori's wrist (Tori's arm must be extended) executes a right snap kick to Tori's stomach (Photo 4); then Uke's right palm sets on Tori's elbow (Photo 5).  Tori's elbow is pushed down, forcing Tori down on his stomach (Photo 6).  Tori's arm must be kept in a vertical position forcing his wrist and taking the knife away.  After the knife is taken away, Tori's arm falls down:  Tori bends his right knee, pulling up under his right armpit, and Tori sits up on his left knee (Photo 7).  Tori slowly pulls his right foot towards his body and stands up.

***Note:***  In the following techniques from # 2 NIHONME to # 10 JUPPONME, the beginning position for Tori is always the left position, except for # 8 and # 9 when Tori is in the right position, at the # 11 and # 12 they are both in Shizentai position.  The Saya remains down.  After every Kata, the knife will be given back to Tori, for the next Kata.  Tori repeats three times, gliding each time at the beginning of each Kata.

Photo 1

Photo 2

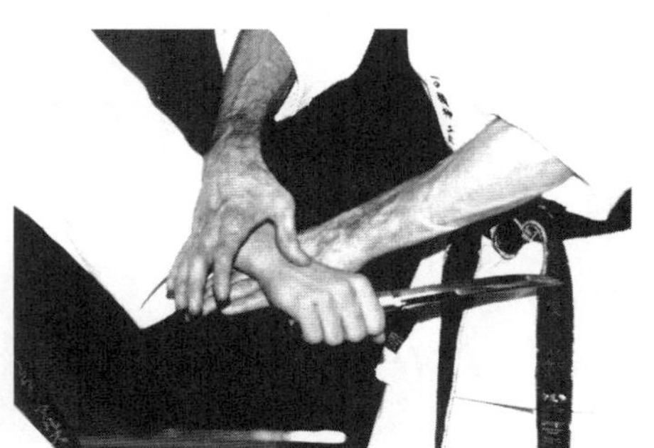

Photo 2a

Photo 2b

Photo 3

Photo 4

Photo 5

Photo 6

Photo 7

### 2. *NIHONME* (Photos 8 to 14a)

Starting position is the same as in # 1. IPPONME.  Tori steps forward into a right position and stabs Uke in the same manner as # 1. IPPONME (Photo 8).  Both combatants have their right leg forward.  Uke tries to catch Tori's stabbing arm; Tori pulls back fast his arm and changes his attack, he drops his arm (Photo 9) and, with a rotative motion from down to up and from the left to the right and then from right to the left, he tries to stab Uke's left side of the neck (Photo 10).

Uke glides a very little towards Tori and defends with a parry with his right palm Tori's forearm and, at the same time, Uke lifts up his left elbow under Tori's right wrist supporting, even closing, the attacker's arm (Photo 10).  Now Uke's right palm slides upwards and catches the back of Tori's palm and lifts up the arm, holding it firmly with the right palm (Photo 11).

Uke steps forward with his right leg diagonally to his right (Photo 11a), then steps forward with his left leg and pushing Tori's elbow down and forward (Photo 12), throwing him, (Photo 13) and landing Tori on his back.  Uke forcing Tori's arm and holding it vertically, now sets his left leg close to Tori's right shoulder turning him on his abdomen (Photo 14).  Tori's arm is controlled by Uke's left leg (Uke's left knee pushes Tori's elbow) (Photo 14a).

Uke takes out the knife from Tori's hand and steps back diagonally in a fighting position.  Tori bends his left knee pulling up under his left armpit and sits up on his right knee. Tori slowly pulls his left foot towards his body and stands up.

Photo 8

Photo 9

Photo 10

Photo 11

Photo 11a

Photo 12

Photo 13

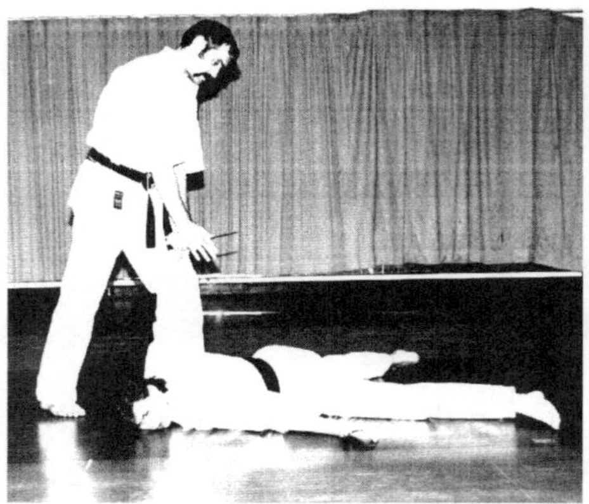
Photo 14

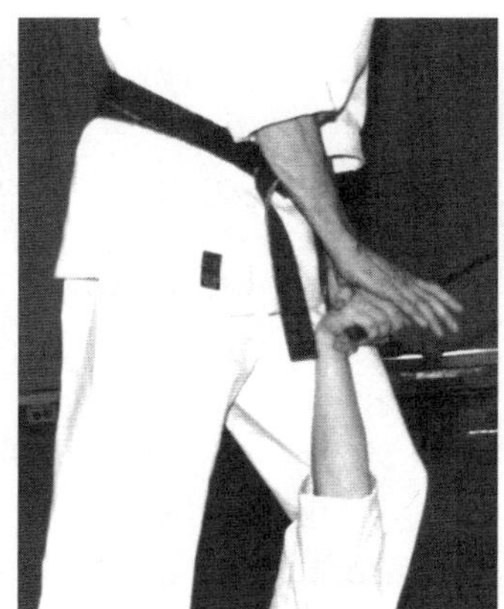
Photo 14a

### 3. *SANBONME* (Photos 15 to 24)

Starting position is the same as in # 1. IPPONME (Photo 1 or 15).  Tori has the knife in his right hand.  He steps forward with his right leg executing a circular stabbing feint from the right to the left into Uke's left ribs, then suddenly changes the knife from his right into his left hand (Photo 16) and steps with the left leg forward.  Now, with the same stabbing motion like before, tries to stab Uke's right side in the ribs (Photo 17).  Uke holds the right position and, at the same time, blocks the attack with Migi Gedan Uke (Photo 17).  (During the block Uke's elbow is lifted up).  Within a 1/4 second, Uke grabs Tori's wrist with his left hand (Photo 18) and, at the same time, he punches Tori's face with his right fist.  (The punching action is not shown in the photo).

Uke, still holding Tori's left wrist with his left arm, steps with his left leg forward to his right between his right leg and Tori's left leg (Photo 19), lifting up Tori's left arm, turning it 180 degrees angle to the right, throwing Tori onto his back (Photos 20, 21).

*Note:*  At the same time before making the 180 degrees angle turn, Uke also catches Tori's wrist with his right hand.  Tori's back fist is being wrapped around by Uke's right palm, and Uke's left palm is above Tori's palm part (inside fist) (Photo 20).

Uke's palms are oriented forward and down (Photo 20).  Uke pushes more with his right heel of the palm against Tori's back fist, forcing Tori to open his fist.  Tori will be rolled over to his left side onto his back.  When Tori is on his back, Uke pushes with his right knee Tori's elbow pressing with both palms Tori's back fist (Photo 22).  Uke pushes Tori's elbow even more and takes the knife away from Tori (Photo 23).  Tori will be pushed onto his stomach, with Uke controlling him with his left palm, and meanwhile leaning on his left knee (Photo 24).

Photo 15

Photo 16

Photo 17

Photo 18

Photo 19

Photo 20

Photo 21

Photo 22

Photo 23

Photo 24

### 4. *YONHONME* (Photos 25 to 33)

Starting position is the same as in # 1. IPPONME (Photo 1).  Tori holds the knife with the blade downward (the blade is at the small finger part of the fist and the edge looks towards Uke).  Tori steps forward into a right position and, during this step, he tries to slash Uke's left forearm from the right to the left (Photo 25).  Uke holds his left forearm pretty highly positioned for distracting Tori's attention (Photo 26).  (During the slashing motion by Tori, Uke avoids just by sliding back easily and pulling his left forearm close to him).  When Tori sees that he missed Uke's left forearm, he tries to stab Uke's chest in a forward motion (Photo 27).

Uke blocks the stabbing action by blocking with a Hidari Jodan Uke (Photo 27) and, at the same time, he executes a Migi Jodan Ura Zuki to Tori's chin.  (This punch is not shown). After the Ura Zuki execution, Uke grabs with his right palm Tori's right wrist (Photo 28).  Uke now executes an Aikido technique Gokyo - negative action (Photo 29).  Tori will not be down on his stomach as, usually, the Gokyo technique requires instead, however, he will be on his back, because Uke pushes with his left knee Tori's right popliteal space and pulls Tori's collar backward with his left arm (Photo 30).  Finally, Tori will be on his left side of the body (Photo 31).  Uke forces Tori's whole arm for knife release with his right knee (Photo 32).  Uke now holds the knife and he is ready to stab Tori (Photo 33).

Photo 25

Photo 26

Photo 27

Photo 28

Photo 29

Photo 30

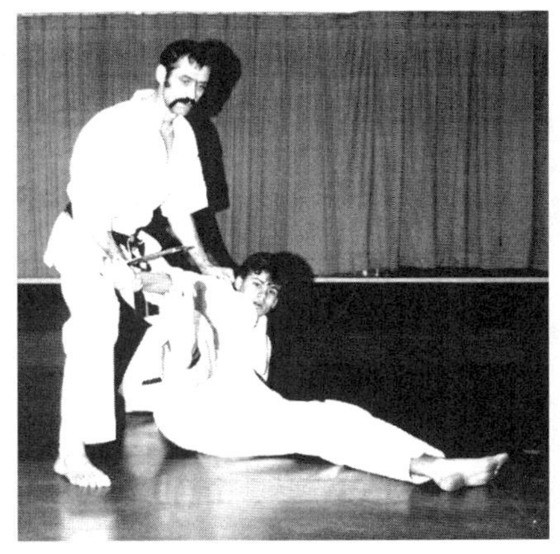

Photo 31       Photo 32       Photo 33

### 5.  *GOHONME* (Photos 34 to 39)

Starting position is the same as in # 1. IPPONME (Photo 1).  Tori steps forward with his right leg and tries to slash Uke's left forearm from the left to the right (Photo 34) (Tori again holds the knife as a sword), then immediately tries to stab Uke's stomach (Photo 35).  Uke defends by stepping back with his left leg and executes a double block (Photo 35).  (Uke defends like in # 1. IPPONME).  Uke lifting up and twists Tori's wrist from left to right (Photo 36).  Uke now releases his right arm and gives pressure with his forearm against the inside part of Tori's elbow (Photo 37).  Uke applies more pressure against Tori's arm, forcing him down on the ground (Photo 38), then pressing, with his right knee, Tori's elbow and also pressing Tori's backhand, forcing him into giving up the knife (Photo 39).

Photo 34       Photo 35       Photo 36

Photo 37                    Photo 38                    Photo 39

### 6. *ROPPONME* (Photos 40 to 51)

The positions and the first attack are like the positions and attack in # 1. IPPONME (Photos 40, 41).  Uke blocks with Gedan Juji Uke (Photo 41).  Tori pulls back his stabbing arm (Photo 42) and launches again another attack, at this time trying to stab straight towards Uke's heart (the execution is similar to that of foil fencers thrust) (Photo 43).  Uke dodges his body to his right, twisting his torso to the left, and blocking this way:

The stabbing arm is blocked practically with his left forearm, with the palm opened, the elbow up and the forearm looking down.  The right forearm follows this block with the right elbow down, and with the palm upwards towards Tori's forearm (Photo 43).  Now the right forearm is practically above the left forearm.  After contact is made with Uke's left forearm against Tori's forearm, Uke catches it with his elbow joint (Photo 44).

Uke's right palm edge follows the action controlling Tori's elbow because Tori's arm will be forced to turn upwards (Photo 45).  Uke is pulling to his right Tori's body, with Tori's head leading down and close to the ground (Photo 46).

Suddenly, Uke's right edge of the palm (Shuto) pushes forward (opposite to the previous action).  Tori's elbow joint is forced and he will fall backward on his back (Photo 47). Uke is still holding Tori's wrist and controlling his elbow joint.  Uke now sitting down on his right knee (Photo 48), catches with his right hand Tori's knife holding hand (Photo 48) and twists it to his right.  Uke's left palm slides upwards to catch Tori's hand and then he stands up (Photo 49).  Uke takes out the knife with his right hand (Photo 50) and slashes, or stabs, Tori's chest (Photo 51).

Photo 40

Photo 41

Photo 42

Photo 43

Photo 44

Photo 45

Photo 46

Photo 47

Photo 48

Photo 49

Photo 50

Photo 51

### 7. *SHICHIHONME* (Photos 52 to 63)

Starting position is the same as in # 1. IPPONME (Photo 1).  Tori steps forward with his right leg and tries to slash Uke's left forearm from the left to the right (Photos 52, 53).  Tori's first and second action is the same as in # 5. GOHONME.  However, instead of stabbing Uke's stomach, Tori tries to stab Uke's neck on the left side.  Uke steps back with his left leg, blocking with his left palm, while punching Tori's chin at the same time with Migi Ura Zuki (Photo 54).

Uke grabs Tori's right wrist (Photo 55) and steps with his right leg in front of Tori's right leg and under Tori's right arm (Photo 56).  He executes an Aikido technique, Uchi Kaiten Sankyo, then pulls Tori's arm backward with both hands forcing his shoulder and creating pain for him (Photo 57).  Then Uke returns Tori's arm towards his chest in such a way that Tori's right arm with the knife goes directly against his chest (Photos 58, 59).  After stabbing Tori's chest, Uke forces him to fall on his back (Photo 60).

Uke controls Tori's arm in such a way that it is forced outside to the right and controlled with Uke's left arm (Photo 61).  Uke grabs the knife from Tori with a twisting motion (Photos 62, 63).

Photo 52

Photo 53

Photo 54

Photo 55          Photo 56          Photo 57

Photo 58          Photo 59          Photo 60

Photo 61          Photo 62          Photo 63

### 8. *HACHIHONME* (Photos 64 to 68)

Starting position is the same as in # 1. IPPONME (Photo 1) or Tori holds the right position, slides forward and tries to slash Uke's right forearm.  Uke defends by pulling back his arm (Photo 64).  Tori changes the slashing motion by stabbing Uke's stomach.  (This action executed with a little bit circular motion from Tori's right to Tori's left and from down to upwards) (Photo 65).  Uke with his right back hand (Haishu) defends outside of Tori's right forearm (Photo 66).  During this action (about Uke's Haishu block), the parry is made with a sliding motion on Tori's forearm, followed by Uke opening wide his thumb and forefinger and grabbing Tori's wrist with the help of his left palm (Photo 67), throwing Tori with an Aikido technique - wrist out-turn throw - (Kote Gaeshi) (Photo 68).

Photo 64

Photo 65

Photo 66

Photo 67

Photo 68

### 9. *KYUHONME* (Photos 69 to 81)

Starting position is the same as in # 1. IPPONME (Photo 1) or both can be in right position. Tori holds the knife as in # 4. YONHONME, with the blade downwards. Tori attempts a slash against Uke's right forearm from the right (Tori's right) to the left (Photo 69). When Tori sees that he missed Uke's right forearm, he then tries to stab Uke's face, which will be blocked by Uke's right forearm (Photo 70). Tori attempts another stab to Uke's ribs, which is blocked with a Migi Gedan Uke (Photo 71). At the same time, Uke grabs Tori's right wrist with his left palm and punches with his right fist Tori's face (Photo 72) (The grabbing left palm of Uke is upwardly oriented) (Photo 72a). Uke firmly holds Tori's right wrist, stepping with his left leg in front of Tori and to the right lifting up Tori's right arm (Photo 72b).

Uke now turns to his right, stepping under Under Tori's right arm and turning his body 180 degrees angle. Uke lifts up his right arm and sets his right shoulder under Tori's right elbow, which will serve as a fulcrum after this, pressing Tori's forearm down with his left palm (Photo 73).

Uke now eliberates his right arm (still holds firmly Tori's right wrist with his left palm) and surrounds Tori's arm (bend of elbow) (Photos 74, 75).  Uke forces Tori's arm by pressing it with the left palm down and with his right arm pressing it upwards (Photos 75a, 75b), by this combined action Tori will be forced down onto his back (Photo 76).  Uke will take the knife with his left hand (Photo 77) and, at the same time, Uke's right arm will slide down holding Tori's right backhand (Photo 78).

Tori tries to liberate himself from this controlled position by turning to his right onto his stomach (Photos 79, 80) and standing up for a complete liberation (Photo 81).  Uke still has the choice of stabbing or throwing Tori away.

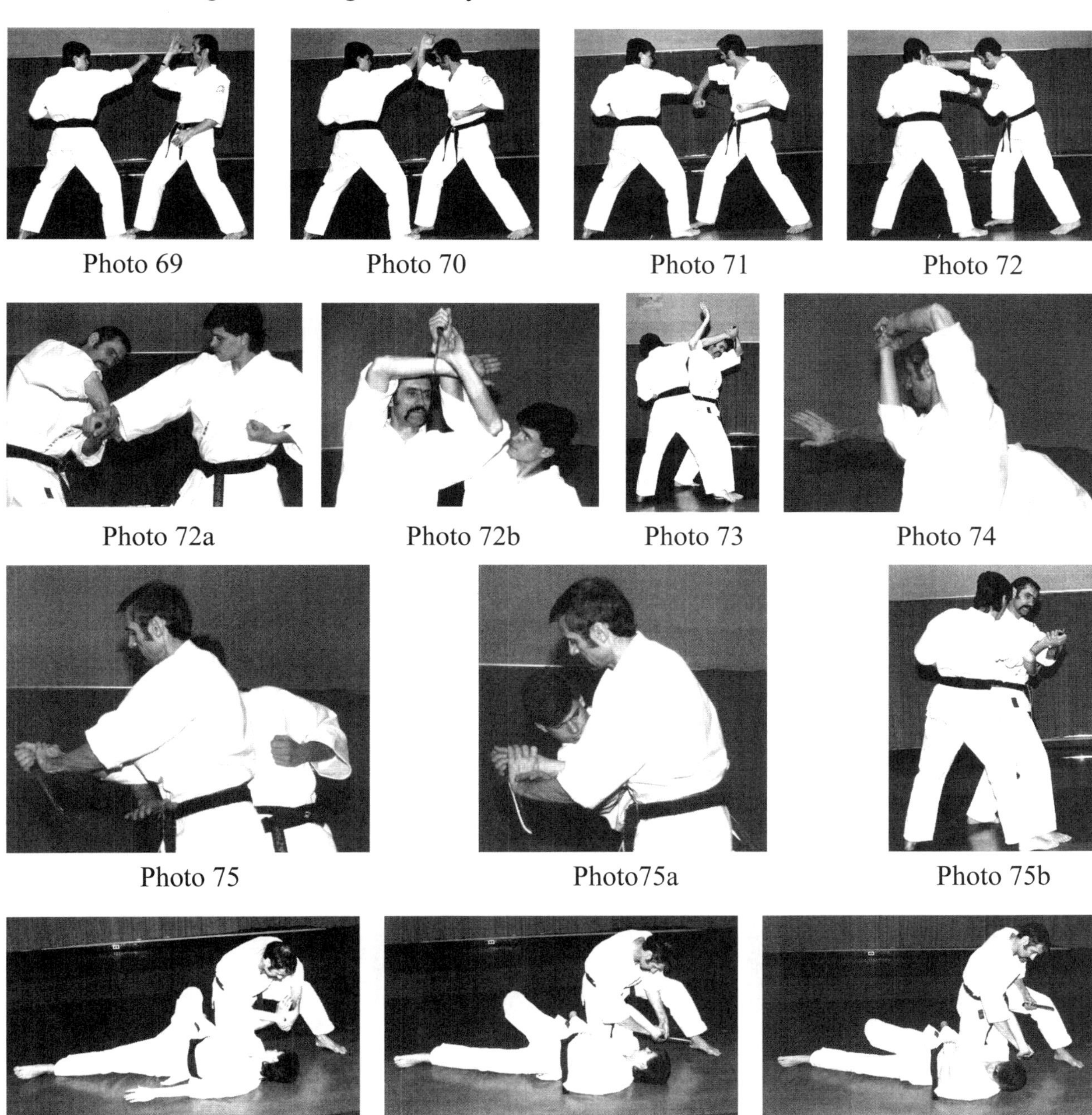

Photo 69     Photo 70     Photo 71     Photo 72

Photo 72a     Photo 72b     Photo 73     Photo 74

Photo 75     Photo75a     Photo 75b

Photo 76     Photo 77     Photo 78

Photo 79

Photo 80

Photo 81

### 10. *JUPPONME* (Photos 82 to 90)

Both Tori and Uke are with their left leg in front (Photo 82).  Tori steps forward trying to slash Uke's left forearm.  Uke pulls back his forearm defending himself (Photo 83) and holding his left position.  Tori now steps forward with his left leg (Photo 84) and tries to stab straight into Uke's ribs.

Uke defends easily sliding with both of his legs to his right side and a little bit backwards and, at the same time, stops Tori's attack with a left side kick to Tori's neck (Hidari Yoko Geri Keage Kekomi) (Photo 85).  This side kick will surprise Tori.  Uke now snaps down his kicking leg outside of Tori's left leg, grabbing Tori's left empty arm with his right hand at the wrist and pushing Tori's chin backwards and down with the heel of his left palm (Shotei) (Photos 86, 86a).  Tori is forced to fall down on his back (Photo 87) and will be pulled onto his stomach (Photos 88, 89), where Uke will bend Tori's left forearm onto Tori's back (Photo 90). From here Uke, pressing Tori's elbow and causing pain, commands Tori (who is in pain) to pull out from under his stomach the knife which he is holding in his right arm.  And now Uke easily can take the knife away from Tori.

Photo 82

Photo 83

Photo 84

Photo 85

Photo 86

Photo 86a

Photo 87

Photo 88

Photo 89

Photo 90

### 11.  *JUIPPONME* (Photos 91 to 95)

Tori attacks Uke from behind.  Tori surrounds, with his left arm, Uke's left shoulder and grabs Uke's left, or right lapel, close to Tori's neck.  Tori sets the edge of the knife against the front of Uke's neck (Tori's right arm is above Uke's right shoulder) (Photo 91).  Uke turns to his left and, suddenly, grabs with his right hand Tori's right hand on the wrist (Photo 92).  Uke, now almost face to face with Tori, lifts up Tori's right arm and crosses Tori's arm (Photo 93).

Uke pushes, with the edge of his left palm, Tori's elbow and makes a stamping kick with the edge of his left foot (Sokuto) (Photo 94).  He forces Tori on the ground (Photo 95), maintaining Tori's right arm in an extended position.  Uke can now twist Tori's wrist and take the knife away.

Photo 91

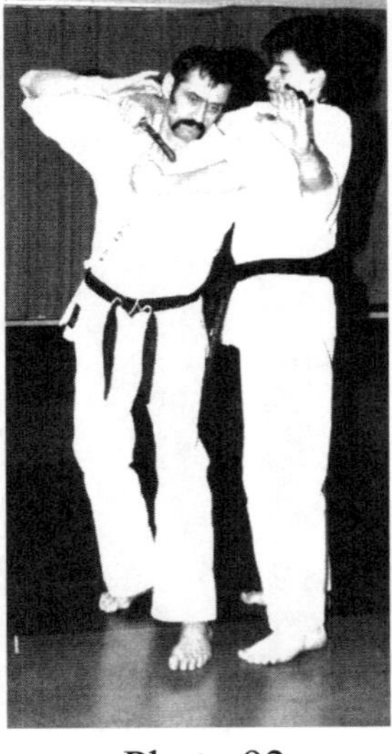

Photo 92

Photo 93

Photo 94

Photo 95

### 12. *JUNIHONME* (Photos 96 to 101)

Tori attacks Uke from behind. Tori grabs, with his left hand, Tori's collar behind the neck, and the right hand, holding the knife, pushes into Uke's spine (Photo 96). Uke turns to his right side, dropping down his right arm, blocking and pushing Tori's knife holding arm to Uke's right (Photo 97). Uke continues turning to the right applying his left palm to Tori's chin and pulling it to Tori's left (Photo 98), forcing Tori to fall on his back (Photo 99). During Tori's fall, Uke instantly grabs Tori's wrist first with his right palm (Photo 99), then with his left palm (Photo 100), pushes with his right knee Tori's right elbow, forcing Tori on his stomach, (Photo 101) forcing him to give up the knife.

Photo 96

Photo 97

Photo 98

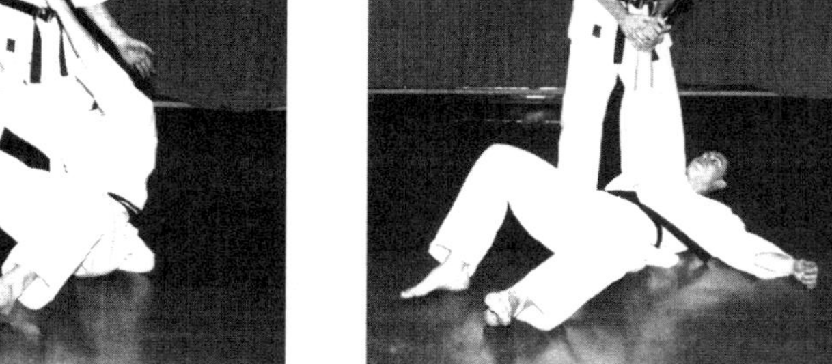

Photo 99                    Photo 100                    Photo 101

Prof. Arus on left sitting, poses with Korean Judo master, Hang Chiang Hi 6th Dan
Kodokan Judo (1976 -1979), standing another Romanian Judo coach

Prof. Arus practicing Aikido (Taninzu Dori) in 1970's

# 8.6.  *FIGHTING (Kumite) RULES IN SENDO-RYU KARATEDO STYLE*

Due to the fact that this style is strongly oriented toward self-defense and not just for sport Karate, any takedown will have a special attention.

- The Jiyu Kumite time is two or tree minutes.
- Points obtained during the match are cumulative (the one with more points is declared the winner).  In case of a draw, the Kumite is prolonged one more minute. Once again, in a draw situation, the more aggressive, more active and technically more accurate Karateka will be declared the winner.


**Black belt level fighting rules**

- Skin touch contact to the face (Jodan) is permitted.
- Full contact to the stomach, chest (Chudan) is permitted.
- No contact at all:  To the neck (front, side and back), to the kidneys, or to the spine.
- Prohibited is the use of finger in attack (Nukite) techniques.
- Using the heel (Kakato), there is very light contact to the Chudan and no contact to the Jodan.
- Elbow (Empi) attacks are controlled to the Jodan and light touch to the Chudan.
- Knee (Hiza) attacks just with control.
- Under the belt level, there is no touching at all to the opponent's knees and shin except for light contact to the side of the calves (inside and outside) and to the side of the thigh (outside).
- Takedown action is two (2) points.
- Punch action or kick action is one (1) point for each.
- Knifehand (Shuto) attacks are permitted just with control.  Any imitation of an attack to the groin is prohibited.
- Takedown follow up with a correct punch or kick is a victory.  (Absolutely light touch on body or control to the head, when the opponent is down).
- Holding is permitted for two (2) seconds, plus another one (1) second for execution of sweeping.
- Knockdown for less than ten (10) seconds is three (3) points.
- Knockout for ten (10) seconds is a victory (knockout not on the face).

# 9.  *COMPETITION (Shiai)*

Shiai is very much like Jiyu Kumite.  Both are types of free fighting with some rules to keep in mind.  It is well known that, in competition, judges and referees adjudicate victory or defeat.  The competition (Shiai) is an important test which shows the general knowledge of the Karateka.  It is also a very important test that shows the combatants ability (when one needs proof), of knowledge using Karate techniques for self-defense purposes.

Shiai is a real fight, especially when the techniques are executed with full contact on the opponents body.  Of course, a better test that shows how well you can be protected in a self-defense situation, using Karate knowledge, would be in a real street fighting situation.

If you are a decent and good human being you will try your best to keep out of trouble as best you can.  And you'll try not to fight and to avoid trouble because, otherwise, you can increase your chances of getting hurt, or arrested by the police.

So what is the best way to test your self-defense ability.  I can positively say that is in sport competition.  Even if you can not kick under the belt and can not use finger tip attacks, or other dangerous techniques, the Shiai is still closer to a street fighting situation than the so called self-defense training that is advocated by the so-called "Peaceful Karate Masters".  These Peaceful Karate Masters say that you don't need Shiai, in order to be efficient in self-defense.

What do they mean by this ?  They teach that any kicking, punching and striking technique should be executed in such a way so as to not harm the partner (even a punch to the abdomen).  This means that if you are trained by this method of caring for your partner, then you will never be able to really hit when you need to, because that is the way that you were trained.  At the beginning of this book I have mentioned about non-contact Karate systems, where the attack is focused and stopped just in front of the opponent.  This is a sublimation of your impulses.  This method helps you to have a better mental attitude and control for your actions.  So, which Karate is better, the non-contact, contact, or full-contact method ?

The answer is simple.  Because each street fight, or each competition, or each opponent is different, the best method is to use a combination of the three in order to think better, to judge better and to fight better.  (All of them to be used in different level of knowledge of the student).

Sendo-Ryu Karatedo uses basically the non-contact and contact Karate method (non-contact for children, contact for adults beginner and intermediate level) and, for the more advanced, particularly the black belts, accent is put on the full contact method to the stomach, chest, ribs, thighs, arms, but excluding the very important vital points, such as the kidney, spine, front of the neck, groin etc.

In Sendo-Ryu Karatedo, the training protocol is made in such a way that, when the Karateka reaches the black belt level and he is fighting with another black belt and they both have the same level of expertise and weight, then both Karateka should resist against any powerful kick or punch directed to the body's midsection area.

**Advice for competition (Shiai)**

– Keep your eyes open, try to look through your opponent's body.  This concept helps you observe your opponent's intentions.
– Keep your stomach tight when you perform, attack, or defend, even when you walk or shift the body.
– Never dash forward at your opponent at the beginning of the match (Hajime).
– Avoid retreating in a straight line.
– When you are retreating, throw a few punches, or kicks, even if they are far from your opponent, because these actions will disturb your opponent.
– When you have finished your attack, be prepared to block any possible counterattacks.
– Never attack without a precise goal and, if so, take up defensive tactics.
– In a three full point system match (Sanbon Shobu), try to score first which is a considerable advantage.
– Alternate the use of kicks and punches (high and low) combination techniques.
– When you are ready to use your favorite fast technique, you should use some slow feints or techniques first.

Soke Arus practicing Iaijutsu

A perfect sidekick executed by Prof. Emeric Arus on right side in
1970's Jiyu Kumite practice

# III

# KARATE TRAINING METHOD AND PERIODS OF PREPARATION

# General principles

Any sport training is systematically developed and continually graduated through the teaching process of adaptation of the human body to intensify physical and psychological efforts, in order to obtain high results in one of the competitive forms of physical exercises.

Generally speaking, this training process has two parts - aspects:

a) Technical      - tactical parts

b) Conditioning  - general physical training parts

                 - specific physical training parts

These two inseparable parts are valid also for Karate training. Sometimes Karate training contains more technical aspects which fit more the beginners and, sometimes, the Karate training contains more conditioning aspects which could fit more advanced athletes. These aspects depend upon the annual training periods which are established by the Karate instructor at the end of each year.

The training period is a subdivision of the annual working - fitting program, including a succession of stages, set in a concrete form by objectives and a special content.

In the annual training program four (4) periods are stipulated.

A) Preparatory period

B) Precompetitional period

C) Competitional period

D) Transition period

These four periods are good for a beginner, who has one or a maximum of three competitions in a given year. Let's say those competitions are in October and in November, and we start the training in January, then the annual periods are:

A) Preparatory period = 8 months (January through August)

B) Precompetitional period = 1 month (September)

C) Competitional period = 2 months (October and November)

D) Transition period = 1 month (December)

The annual training program can also have two precompetitional periods of two weeks each, before each competitional period. For athletes with more than three years preparation - accumulated experience, and more than 6-8 competitions/year, the annual periods could be different in the following way. The instructor establishes the athlete's preparations for the most important competition of the year, where the athlete should be at the maximum peak of his physical, physiological and mental preparation.

Let's say, if the most important competition is in June every year, then we can set up the annual training program from May to May or from June to June.

Let's assume that the Karateka has 6 years experience in Karate training, and he is already a national champion in his division, and the sport events calendar is as follows:

– June 4, 2000 - Selection competition (trial) for representing the country in July 2001 at the World Championships (No participation for this trial selection).
– July 2, 2000 - Tristate tournament - No participation.
– August 2000 - No competitions.
– September 2000 - One competition - No participation.
– October 2000 - Three competitions - Participation at one of the tournaments.
– November 2000 - One competition - Participation - Objective: The Karateka should be between the first three (first, second or third place).
– December 2000 - No competitions.
– January 2001 - Regional tournament - Participation - Objective: The Karateka must win this tournament.
– February 2001 - One local competition - Must participate and obtain at least third place.
– March 2001 - Two local competitions - Must participate.
– April 2001 - No competitions.
– May 2001 - Two competitions - Must participate - must win one and should take at least a second place in other competition.
– June 2001 - Selection competition (trial) for World Championships in July 6-8, 2001 - Participation and must win in a very categorical manner.

Now you can see, that as the more important Karate competitions approach, the Karateka must win, or at least he should take 2nd or 3rd place. Using this sport event calendar, the annual training period could be as follows:

– June 4, 2000 to October. 2000 = Preparatory period (The first one).
– November 2000 = Precompetitional and competitional period (The first week is precompetitional and the last three weeks for competitional period).
– December 2000 = Transition period (The first one).
– January 2001 to April 2001 = Preparatory period (The second one).
– May 1, 2001 to June 10, 2001 = Precompetitional period (The second one).
– June 10, 2001 to July 8, 2001 = Competitional period (The second one).
– The transition period is after the World Championships (The second one).

### *What should the Karateka do in these periods ?*

During the preparatory period, the athlete should be working on his general physical conditioning (14). He should also be working on his technical Karate knowledge, especially concentrating on basic techniques (Kihon), along with a lot of repetition.

During conditioning, the Karateka should work at least 2 - 4 times a week for running, weight lifting and improving his endurance. The preparatory period is characterized by long periods of working for improving cardio-vascular and aerobic systems of the body. This period is characterized as a monotonous work-out and is done on quantity bases, such as lessons that are longer in time 2 - 2 1/2 hours more, where the effort is based upon endurance, and the Karate techniques work-out are based on knowledge accumulation.

The ***precompetitional period*** is the most difficult period.  This period should be guided in multi directional facets.  This period contains all the technico-tactical parts of the Karate training, as well as the conditioning aspects of the training.  Conditioning should be also specific to the Karate training and, during this period, the instructor should try to bring the athlete's physical, physiological and mental preparation to a submaximal level of effort.

The Karateka should be working on combination techniques and tactics, and the emphasis should be on speed.  The work load should be more for quality, speed (explosive power), with training periods shorter in time, and with training work-outs whose intensity are submaximal (85 % to 100 % is a maximal work-out).

Instructors should guide their athletes by informing them about adequate nutritional substances, including the correct dosage of proteins, fats, carbohydrates, vitamins and minerals.

The ***competitional period*** is characterized by athletic training, which consists of submaximal and maximal effort.  The working profile focuses on specific aspects of Karate training.  Karate combinations and tactics are the most important tasks in this training period. The repetitions are made with maximum speed.  The athlete should have enough Kumite experience, but with special concern on preventing accidents since, if they were to happen even once, they could possibly diminish the athlete's top performance or state.

Basically, the athletic maximal shape can be maintained for 2 - 4 weeks, for most times just for three weeks.  During this period, the athlete should maintain a submaximal effort of training near maximal effort, between 75 % to 95 % of his maximal possibility for a work-out.

During the ***transition period***, the Karateka should practice other sport as complementary exercises, and he should rest more.  In this period he should train 2 - 3 times per week 1 hour or 1 hour and 15 minutes with very reduced volume and intensity.  A top Karateka should practice basketball, soccer, swimming etc.  Also, he should find recreational activities, as fishing, hunting, horse riding etc.

Special attention should be given to those athletes who work with 88 % to 100 % of their maximal potential, so as to make sure that these athletes do not enter in a so-called overtraining (staleness) state (15).

***The organization of training process should include the following aspects:***

**A)  Planning records**
- Long term plan (the following years, usually for 3 - 4 years)
- Yearly plan (the current year)
- Periodic or monthly plan (includes more weeks - usually four weeks)
- Weekly plans (includes number of trainings for the current week)
- Lesson plan (includes warm-up, basic training, cool-down part descriptions)

***Long term plan*** should include methodological orientation for the future, intermediate and final performance objectives, testing dates, different kinds of tests (e.g., push-ups, running, weight lifting, rope jumping test - how long period the Karateka can skip, fight against two or more opponents), the optimal numbers of competitions, organizational, administrative and budget planning for equipments, allocation for traveling, main tournaments dates etc.

***Yearly plan*** should include final results from events from previous years, methodological orientation regarding the progress of the effort (volume, intensity and complexity), intermediate and final performance objectives, sports events calendar, testing dates, dates of medical check ups etc.

***Periodic plan*** should include period amount (number of weeks), objective of the period, effort control (volume, intensity).

***Weekly plan*** should include dates and hours of the trainings, specifications of work load, volume (quantity), intensity (minimal average, submaximal, maximal), work load about the motrical qualities (speed, strength, endurance, ability and mobility indexes).

***Lesson plan*** should include warm-up parts minutes, different exercises, basic part training what kind of techniques will be taught, repetitions, conditioning exercises, work load, what kind of stretching exercise will be used etc.

### B)  File records

Name, addresses, telephone, occupation, birthday, weight, height, belt color or level (Kyu or Dan), date start of Karate, main results of contests or tournaments, health situation, accidents if any, test results, general progress of the Karateka etc.

Soke - Arus executes a legsweeping technique (Ko Uchi Gari)
Opponent - Sensei Emeric Arus Jr.

# IV

# KARATE INJURIES PREVENTION AND TREATMENTS

We know that medicine has two parts:  Prophylactic medicine (preventive) and therapeutic or curative medicine.  Erasmus, a Middle Age surgeon, said in 1508 "Satius est initiis mederi quam fini." (It is better to cure the beginnings than the ends of diseases).

It is important to prevent possible injuries related to Karate, than to treat them later on. Injury treatment costs time and money and is not always 100 % successful.  Here are a few pointers that a coach, organizer, or even Karateka, should take into consideration before starting to practice Karate.

### Before Karate lesson

- Nails should be cut short  (mandatory).
- No earrings allowed        (mandatory).
- Medical check up           (mandatory).
- Not eating 1 hour and 30 minutes or 2 hours before the lesson.
- Body and Karategi must be clean.
- Do not practice Karate if you feel bad (have a nasty cold, or your previous injury did not yet heal).
- Hair should be cut short or should be tied up (mandatory).

Before any Karate competition, one should look for the following problems, in order to prevent possible injuries:

- You as an instructor and a martial artist, should know about rules and regulations. Rules are different in full contact Karate, or no contact Karate competition, and rules are different, and their interpretation, when the fights are done for one or for three points, etc.
- One should not fight with fever for any reason (if one fights with fever one can get into a shock and collapse).
- No fighting with other health related bad symptoms.
- No fighting with an unhealed bruise, blister, abrasion, muscle strain of the IInd or IIIrd degree and ligament sprains of the IInd or IIIrd degree.
- No fighting, if you have to lose too much weight, in order to make it in the category.

Look for hygiene problems:

- Do not fight in dirty, too warm, or too cold places.  The floor should be very clean.
- Do not fight were the illumination is very poor.
- Do not fight when you are very tired.
- Do not fight in very loud and noisy areas with more than 84 - 112 decibels (however you can reduce the noise sensation by meditation - auto-suggestion).
- Do not fight with a Karategi that is too tight or too loose.

If the coach and the athlete takes into consideration these facts, then the injury possibilities can be reduced substantially.

# Injury treatments

A good Karate instructor should have basic knowledge of Cardio-Pulmonary Resuscitation (CPR) procedures.  He should know about the most frequent injuries that have occurred in the Karate field.  There are controversy between specialists on what are the body areas which most frequently are affected by accidents and what kind of accidents they are.  In our opinion, (and the author's personal opinion) there are three areas, with their specific parts, that are frequently affected:

a)  **The head:**  Especially broken nose and bruises around the eyes.
b)  **The body midsection area:**  Especially fractured ribs.
c)  **The groin area:**  Especially the pubis bone fissured or bruised.  Kicking of the testicles happens more with beginners and very seldom with advanced Karateka.

### *Description of the injuries*

### Blisters

Blisters are common injuries.  The skin's surface swells up which is a result of the friction and pressure between the surface of the skin (bare foot) and the hard (wood) floor.  These swollen parts can contain liquid or sometimes blood.  The initial treatment is to stop the training, as soon as possible, to prevent further infection, because the blister can partially or totally rip off, coming in contact with dirt, and infection can occur.

*Treatment:*

If the blister is opened partially with a piece of skin remaining, the opened area should be cleansed with Phisoderm liquid soap (hydrogen peroxide) which is an antiseptic liquid.  Then it should be left to dry completely, set back the remaining skin to its original and anatomical place, apply a wide Band - Aid with a little pressure over the flat area, and then put strip of tape over it.

### Abrasions

This is a superficial skin injury related to a continuous friction of the leg to the floor.  The epidermis of the skin has a scraped look.  If the injury is opened the possibility of infection is obvious.

*Treatment:*

If the injury is not opened, then the injured part should be covered with an antibiotic ointment (Mycitracin) and wrapped with a lightly rolled gauze.

### Contusions (Bruises)

The mechanism that produces it is a blow or strike against soft tissues (especially skin, fat and muscle) compressed against the hard bone underneath.  If the blow is hard enough, capillaries could rupture which, in turn, would allow bleeding into the tissues.  If the bleeding is superficial, then it causes a purple - blue discoloration, which will persist for several days.  Pain also will persist for several days and the discoloration disappears anywhere from 7 to 14 days.

When the contusion occurs, the area swells, and is followed by a bluish discoloration.  Immediately, elastic tape (compressive type) should be applied for compression, then ice should be applied and the injured limb should be elevated against gravity.  By doing this the venous blood will recirculate faster towards the heart.

Whenever superficial tissues, or even deeper tissues, are bleeding, the following process should be applied:

R - Rest (duration depends on the gravity of the accident, can be from 3 to many days - not more than 7 - 10 days).
I - Ice (first 48 - 72 hours), after that, ice should be stopped.
C - Compression for diffusion of liquid and blood.
E - Elevation.

### Muscle strains

The muscle is basically composed of separate fibers that are capable of simultaneous contraction when stimulated by the central nervous system.  Muscles are attached to bone by tendons.  If a muscle is overstretched, or forced to contract against too much resistance, damage occurs to the muscle fibers.  This separation, or tearing, of muscle fibers is referred to as a "Strain".  The muscle and its tendon operate as a single unit, and injury to either part affects the other.

***First-degree strain:***  Some muscle fibers have been stretched.  Active motion produces some tenderness and pain.  Movement is painful, but full range of motion is usually possible.

***Second-degree strain:***  Some muscle fibers have been torn, and active contraction of the muscle is extremely painful.  Usually a palpable depression, or divot, exists somewhere in the muscle belly at the spot where the muscle fibers have been torn.  Some swelling my occur because of capillary bleeding.

***Third-degree strain:***  There is a complete rupture of a muscle in the muscle belly, in the area where muscle becomes a tendon, or at the tendonous attachment to the bone.

*Treatment:*

Treatment of first and second degree injury is directed toward protecting the muscle and tendon from further injury until healing is complete.  Immediate treatment should include ice packs to injured area, followed by a compressive wrap with an elastic-type bandage.  The injured part should be rested.  After the pain and swelling have disappeared, daily stretching and slow contraction of the injured part, along with ice application, will help recovery and maintain function.  A third-degree strain of the muscle necessitates surgical intervention in most cases.

## Ligament sprains

A sprain involves damage to a ligament that provides support to a joint.  A ligament is a tough, relatively inelastic band of tissue that connects one bone to another.  Ligaments are designed to hold two bony areas together at the joints.  All joints are entirely surrounded by a thick ligamentous joint capsule.  The inner surface of this joint capsule is lined by a very thin synovial membrane that is highly vascularized and innervated.  The synovial membrane produces synovial fluid, the functions of which include lubrication, shock absorption, and nutrition of the joint.  If stress is applied to a joint that focuses motion beyond its normal limits or planes of movement, injury to the ligament is likely.

***First-degree sprain:***  There is some stretching, or perhaps tearing, of the ligamentous fibers with little or no joint instability.  Mild pain, little swelling, and joint stiffness may be apparent.

***Second-degree sprain:***  There is some tearing and separation of the ligamentous fibers and moderate instability of the joint.  Moderate to severe pain, swelling, and joint stiffness should be expected.

***Third-degree sprain:***  There is total rupture of the ligament, manifested primarily by gross instability of the joint.  Severe pain may be present initially, followed by little or no pain due to total disruption of nerve fibers.  Swelling may not be profuse and thus the joint tends to become very stiff some hours following the injury.  A third-degree sprain usually requires surgical repair.

*Treatment:*

The treatment of the first-degree sprain usually requires RICE procedures.  The treatment of the second-degree sprain requires more attention, more time for healing and more patience from the athlete.  The healing of the ligament is slow and requires six to eight weeks for complete recovery.  The RICE method must be applied.  Complete immobilization with a plastic cylinder is probably the best treatment of second-degree sprain.

### Fractures

They can be generally classified as being simple (closed) fractures or compound (open) fractures. A compound, or open, fracture involves enough displacement of the fractured ends that the bone actually disrupts the cutaneous layers and breaks through the skin. An increased possibility of infection exists in a compound fracture. In Karate the fractures are mostly simple. And most of the time they are cracked ribs, fractured metacarpien bones and face bone fractures etc.

### Dislocations

Dislocation occurs when at least one bone in an articulation is forced out of its normal anatomical alignment and stays out until it is either manually or surgically put back into place. Dislocations most commonly occur in Karate practice in the elbow, fingers and seldom in the shoulder joint.

*Treatment:*

Treatment should be directed immediately, in order to prevent swelling. Basically, any dislocated anatomical part of the body should be pulled out in an extreme position (hyperextension), then set back to its normal alignment. Followed by the RICE treatment.

## Cardio-Pulmonary Resuscitation (CPR)
(See Fig. 78)

The goal of CPR is to provide oxygen to the brain, heart, and other vital organs until a correct medical treatment can restore normal heart and pulmonary function. This is accomplished by combining external compression of the chest wall with artificial ventilation, mouth-to-mouth resuscitation. If a person's heart, or breathing, has stopped, CPR must be started at once in order to avoid brain damage, which usually begins in 4 to 6 minutes after cardiopulmonary arrest.

First, it must be determined if the person is unconscious. Tap him on the chest gently, shout and shake the shoulders gently. Determine if the person is breathing. If he is breathing, you may assume that his heart is still functioning, because breathing always stops before the heart does. If there is no detectable breathing, check for pulse. If there is weak or absent and no sign of breathing, immediately begin CPR. Three important steps should be kept in mind.

a) The person must be lying flat on the back on a straight, firm surface. Open the airway. During unconsciousness, the tongue relaxes and can block the airway. To clear the airway, place one of your palms across the forehead and, using your other hand lift the neck, or lift the chin, up and forward. At the same time, gently push down on the forehead. This head-tilt, chin lift maneuver forces the epiglottis and tongue away from the airway.

b)  Artificial ventilation is begun using mouth-to-mouth technique.  The rescuer gently pinches the victim's nostrils closed so that air will not escape (the base of this hand is on the forehead).  Then he takes a deep breath, opening his mouth (the rescuer) very wide and placing it around the outside of the victim's mouth, making a seal.

He blows air into the victim's mouth.  Out of the corner of his eye, the rescuer watches to see if the victim's chest is rising.  If it is, the lungs are ventilated.  Adequate ventilation is ensured on every breath by the rescuer making the following observations:

1.  seeing the chest rise and fall;  2.  feeling on his own airway the resistance and compliance of the victim's lungs as they expand;  3.  hearing and feeling the air escape during exhalation.

The initial ventilatory maneuver should be four (4) *quick*, full breath without allowing for full lung collapse between breaths.  After delivering each breath, the rescuer *quickly* turns his head toward the victim's chest to take a breath of fresh air.  Throughout the time of giving the four breaths, positive pressure is maintained in the airway.  If breathing has stopped, even for a short time, some of the small air sacs of the lung collapsed.  These are more efficiently filled and ventilated by maintaining positive pressure in the lungs during the four initial full breaths.  If the heart is still beating this maneuver will restore spontaneous breathing.

c)  Next assess circulation by checking the pulse in the carotid artery.  This is done in 5 to 10 seconds by locating the groove between the trachea and strap muscles - sternocleidomastoid muscle - of the neck.  Press gently to avoid compressing the artery.  If there is no pulse, the diagnosis of cardiac arrest is confirmed and external compression is begun after the initial four breaths.

External chest compression always must be accompanied by artificial ventilation.

### *The procedure of CPR (step-by-step)*

- Establishing unresponsiveness (tap or gently shake and shout).
- Calling out for help.
- Positioning the victim.
- Opening the airway - Head tilt - Neck lift or Head tilt - Chin lift.
- Establishing breathlessness (look, listen, feel).
- Start mouth-to-mouth ventilation, start with the initial four quick full breath.
- Remove your mouth, turn your face toward the person's chest and observe the chest rise outward and hear and feel the air being expelled from the airway.
- Start a rhythmic mouth-to-mouth maneuver of about two forceful breaths with 15 compressions in a single CPR rescuer.
- Establishing presence or absence of pulse.
- Begin chest compression (if pulse absent).
- During two rescuer CPR one breath with 5 chest compression (the breath is interposed during the upstroke of the fifth chest compression), a single rescuer should perform each series of 15 chest compressions at a rate of approximately 80 per minute to deliver close to 60 compressions per minute.  The compression rate for two rescuer is 60 per minute.

- For external cardiac compression the executor (case of single rescuer) should be positioned to the side of the person so that the executor's hand is directly over the midsection of the breastbone, and he should be kneeling if the person is on the floor.
- For compression, place the heel of the hand in the center of the chest over the lower end of the breastbone.  The heel of the other hand is placed on top of the first hand.  Elevate the fingers of both hands, so they do not rest upon the ribs.  With the hand in this position, press downward, using the weight of your upper body, and depress the sternum downward the backbone 1 - 1 1/2 inches.  This external compression, compresses the heart, which is between the sternum and the spine.  After compressing the chest, quickly lift your hands to their original position, allowing the chest to expand the heart to refill with blood.

Important points to remember in performing artificial ventilation and external chest compression:

1) Do not interrupt CPR for more than five seconds, except with problems with transportation.
2) Do not move the patient to a more convenient site until he has been stabilized.
3) Never compress the xiphoid process at the tip of the sternum.
4) Between compressions, the heel of the hand must completely release its pressure but should remain in constant contact with the chest wall.
5) Sudden or jerking movements should be avoided when compressing the chest.  The compression should be smooth, regular, and uninterrupted (50 % of the cycle should be compression, and 50 % should be relaxation).
6) Pressure with fingers on the ribs, or lateral pressure, increases the possibility of rib fractures and costochondral (16) separation.
7) The shoulders of the rescuer should be directly over the victim's sternum.

Cardio Pulmonary Resuscitation

Airway

Tilting the head

Clearing the mouth
and-chin-lift

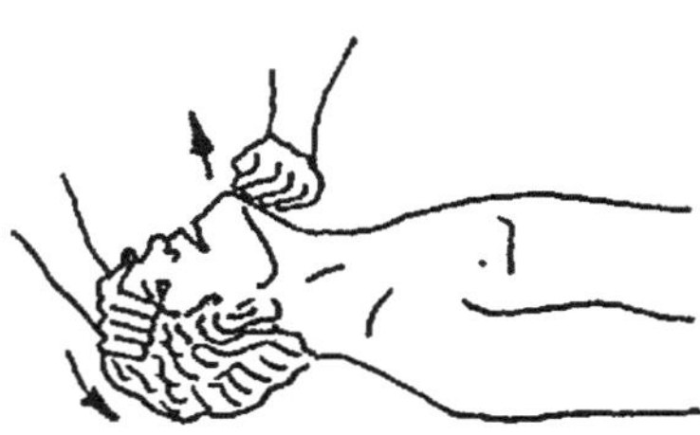

Breathing
Mouth-to-mouth

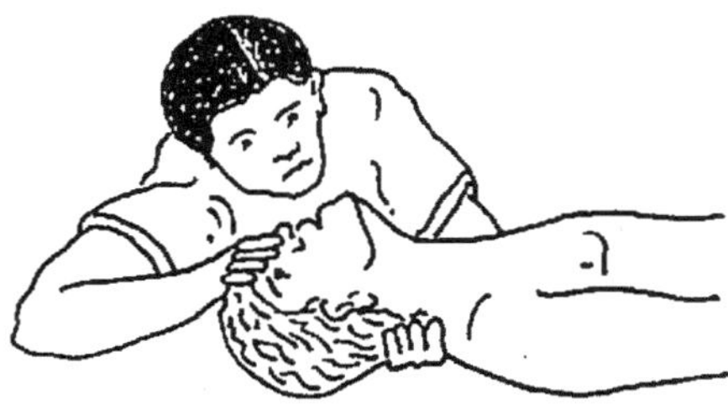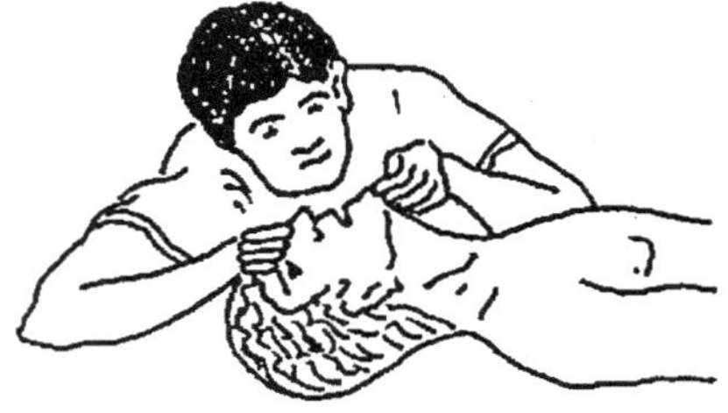

Circulation

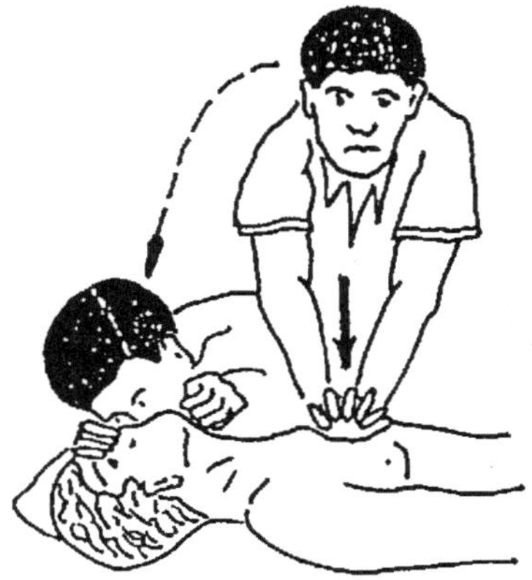

Fig. 78

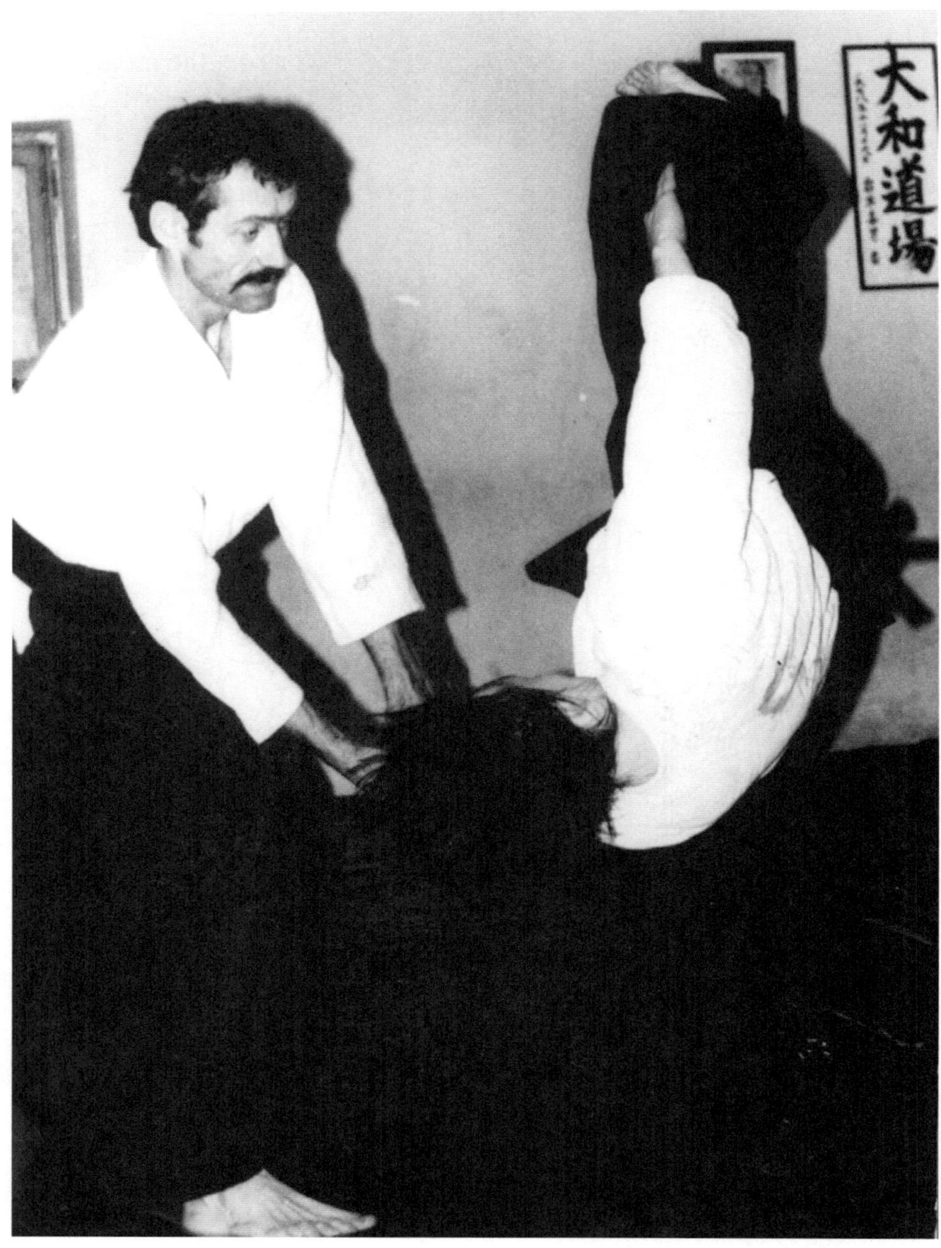

Prof. Arus practicing Aikido (Kote Gaeshi)

# V

## KARATE FOR CHILDREN

## Specific needs and limitations in conditioning and training of children up to 13 years old
(Fig. 79)

In any sport the organized activity (training) requires a selection based on scientific orientation. A good coach must keep track of the following factors:

a)  Age selection
b)  Anatomo-morphological types of selection
c)  Reason for selection
d)  Orientation of the selection

Generally, the selection activities are displayed in three stages:

1) *Preselection* - In Karate activity the preselection takes place during the competitions and demonstrations when the children are attracted by Karate, which can become their preferred sport.

2)  *Selection* (continuous selection) - It is done during the training sessions:  The instructor supervises the children and selects their qualities and habits to build up later a real Karateka.

3)  *Final selection* - It already supposes a certain amount of practice done by children, the coach conducting them towards top performances.  In this stage the training can be individualized and detailed for each athlete.

**The selection factors:**

a)  *Age selection* - In Karate activity, the ideal age is between 7 - 10, when the speed and the ability are well developed, also intelligence, attention, and thinking processes are well developed.  The age between 11 - 13 is even better for starting Karate, but a little late for really top performances.  Now the speed and the skills are developed even more and the mobility of the joints can be extended much more without risks of sprain.

b)  *Anatomo-morphological types of selection* - The children selected must be normally developed physically and mentally.  The tall types (longilin) are preferred.

c)  *Reason for selection* - The coach conducts the training combined with games to capture the children's attention and interests.

d)  *Orientation of the selection* - This factor means that in Karate competing in Kata, in Kumite, or practicing with weapons (Kobudo), or choosing Karate practice for self-defense etc.

The work with children in Karate training (as well as in other individual sports) between the ages 7 - 13 must be multilateral sport preparation.  The relation between general physical preparation (G PH P) and specific physical preparation (S PH P) plus technique (T) must be correctly measured. (See Fig. 79)

During this working period the training can be intensive in speed and ability development, but strength and especially working endurance can be negligible.  During the specific Karate training, general imitative dynamic games are introduced, as well as different games that are appropriate to specific Karate needs.

It is well known that children between 7 - 10 get bored quickly because of repeating the same techniques.  In order to capture their attention and interest, the instructors are advised to introduce games, such as running and jumping for a few minutes, then start to repeat again Karate techniques.  It is very important that the correct combination of quantity and quality be varied as well as the length of the training period.

The first three months of Karate study require slower and more attentive executions in order to assimilate correct techniques.  In the next training period (between 4 - 7 months) the techniques must be executed with much more speed, even if the execution is a little more incorrect.  The techniques are corrected all the time.  The introduction of varied games of running, jumping, fighting has great importance for children in any sport preparation.

(1)  The running, jumping and fighting games offer a great contribution to general physical development which is a base for specific physical development.  This will be a very important factor in the junior and senior ages.

(2)  The fighting games (pulling or pushing partners or different objects) help the development of the fighting spirit.

(3)  The jumping games (on or off the different apparatus - alone or with partners) develop the feeling of the floor, space orientation.

It is highly recommended to work with elastic belts.  They are useful, in general, as well as in specific conditioning and techniques.

*Teaching Kata* - can be done in the usual way introducing new things.  Example:  At the certain Kata, when the Kiai must be executed near the execution spot, the instructor places some object or a red (orange) paper.  This intensifies the Kiai and, of course, the focus (Kime) of the technique.

*Teaching Kihon* is done in the usual way or can be introduced jumping, running exercises or combined with these exercises etc.  For example:  Can be taught double level kick (Nidan Geri), or jumping front kick Mae Tobi Geri.  Even if they are not basic kicks, they also require an ability to learn.  They give pleasure to children because they like to jump, plus this technique helps for a better learning of the basic kicks as Mae Geri.  In the case of Mae Geri, the Nidan Geri helps in the positive transfer of the motor learning.  Other exercises, such as Yoko Geri, can destroy the quality of learning - negative transfer in the motor learning (17).  The Gyaku Zuki punches can be executed even while running (successive punching) etc.

*Teaching Jiyu Kumite* is done in a different way from the usual methods of adult training.  Body protectors can be used, depending on the Jiyu Kumite purpose.  To children, it must be explained that, in Jiyu Kumite, the punches and kicks are stopped a little short of the target.  At the beginning they can fight with the circular techniques which are more visible (Mawashi Geri,  Mawashi Shuto Uchi, Tettsui Uchi etc).  They are less dangerous than straight techniques, such as Tsuki Waza.  The techniques can be executed only in Chudan level etc. Forced preparation brings the children's body to stagnation to such a degree as to make them ill.

The first competition must be minutely prepared.  Research proves that the duration of preparation for the first competition must be at least one year of training.

The proportion between G PH P and S PH P + T:

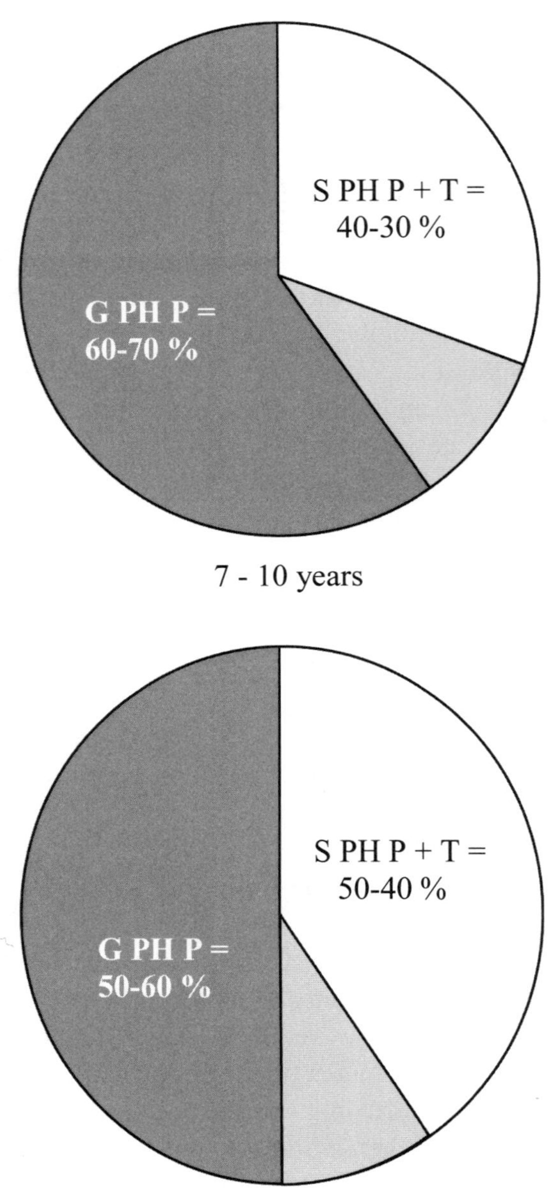



Fig. 79

# VI

## USE OF EQUIPMENT IN KARATE

## General principles of using equipment

Any sport training is a systematically developed and continually enforced pedagogical process of adaptation of the human body to physical and psychical efforts to obtain high results in one of the competitive forms of the physical exercises.

Uses of different equipment, such as specific for Karate training:  Punching board (Makiwara), hanging striking pad (Take Maki), heavy sand bag (Sutanawara), etc. are used to improve the techniques, specific speed, as well as to improve the hitting power and endurance related to a lot of execution.

Use of dumbbells, barbells, jumping ropes, heavy medicine balls, hanged small hitting bags, stone lever weight (Chishi), iron clogs (Tetsu Geta) are used mostly in conditioning training to improve the general speed, general strength, and the general endurance.

These equipments are very important for top athletes.  The various equipments are used all year long, or are used in certain periods of preparation, or combined in one training, which is divided in two parts:

(a) Technico-tactics and  (b) Conditioning.  Scientifically using these equipments must be related with training periods established at the end of each year for the next year.

The training period is a subdivision of the annual training program, including a succession of stages put in a concrete form by objectives and a special content.  For the annual training program, four periods are stipulated (as mentioned in Chapter III).  During the preparatory period, all the equipment, but especially the weights, is used most often, because this period mostly coincides with the conditioning process.

During the precompetitional and competitional periods, the following equipment is frequently used:  Dumbbells, small hitting bags, Makiwara etc., in order to maintain and even to improve the speed and the technical ability.  The leg stretcher is used to improve the flexibility of the joints and elasticity of the muscles.

During the transition period, the athletes rest or practice other complementary sports.  In this period the traditional Okinawan Kobudo weapons can be used, such as:  Nunchaku, Sai, Tonfa, Kama etc., which help to improve the general skill.

### General recommendation and dosage in use of equipment

1) *Punching Board* (Makiwara)

Is used to develop technique, specific speed, specific power and for hardening the natural weapons of the body such as, knuckles of the fist, forearm, elbow, knee etc.  Generally, it is used between 8 - 12 minutes after each training, or to be executed between 60 - 120 times punches or strikes at the surface of the Makiwara.  Under 18 years of age, it is not recommended to be used because it can do damage to the bone growing process.  15 - 20 minutes usage is recommended only for top athletes and not for all trainings.  The Makiwara is the most specific equipment for Karate training.  The rigid Makiwara, which is fixed to the wall, is not recommended for use.

The use of rigid Makiwara can do damage to wrist or elbow joints and also to tendons.

2) *Heavy sand bag* - over 40 lb (Sutanawara)

It is especially used to develop strength.  Because the Karateka moves around the bag, the use of this equipment also creates the feel of distance (Ma Ai).  It can be used as many times as possible for hands and legs.  The heavy bag is the main tool for hardening the instep, shin, elbow and knee.

3) *Barbells and Olympic weights* - over 150 lb.

Are used for general conditioning to develop the athlete's muscles and especially strength.  It can be used after every training, or periodically (especially during the preparatory periods).  If the athlete wants to develop his maximum strength, he must work with 70 - 100 % weights to his maximum capabilities.  For endurance, it is used 35 - 55 % from the maximum possibility of the athlete.  Also the dumbbells are used repeatedly.  For speed development, the exercises with dumbbells are very useful, but the exercises must be executed very rapidly.

4) *Jumping rope*

Generally, it is used to maintain or develop the general endurance.  It is also useful for general ability and can be used as many times and as much as the athlete wants to.  It can be used during the lesson period, but it is used generally in warm ups, or cool downs, or in special work out sessions.  It is recommended to be used for 5 - 15 minutes with series of 5 minutes and a rest of 1 - 2 minutes between them.

5) *Elastic cord* (rubber rope) (Fig. 80)

This is an extraordinary equipment which can be used for general conditioning, as well as for specific conditioning.  Examples:
a)  The Karateka is in Hidari Zenkutsu Dachi (Fig.80), one end of the elastic cord is fixed behind him, usually at his belt level or lower, the other end of the cord is held by his right fist.  The Karateka executes Gyaku Zuki.  The distance can be extended or shortened from the fixed point.  This is up to the Karateka's muscular potential.  If the cord is in a relaxed position, then the execution must be emphasized for speed (more repetition); if the cord is more extended, the execution must be emphasized more for strength (slow executions). If the Karateka can maintain the maximum extended position 6 - 12 seconds, the exercise already receives the isometric aspect.
b)  The Karateka is in same position, but now his right ankle is fixed behind by the cord and the exercise is useful for kicks.  The elastic cord can also be used for other executions, such as Uraken Uchi, Kizami Zuki, Yoko Geri etc.

Note:

More precaution is needed when the elastic cord is completely extended, because it can be retracted very fast and can cause damage to the athlete's muscles, such as overextension of the tendons, muscle strains, ligament sprains etc.

6) *Iron clogs* (Tetsu Geta)

It is used to develop legs, but especially abdominal muscles.

7) *Stone lever weight* (Chishi)

It is used to develop complete upper body muscles especially chest, shoulder and forearm muscles.

Fig. 80

## Appendix A:  Author's advice for practicing Karate

The best advice to start practicing Karate is to try to read a little bit about Karate and other martial arts.  Also, visit several martial arts exhibitions which include Karate, Judo, Aikido, Jujitsu, Kung-Fu etc.  It is impossible to understand these martial arts' philosophies in a short period of time, but look to those who practice these arts and try to adopt to your benefit the physical, mental and spiritual traits that the arts provide.

The second step should be to visit several Dojo-s, watch their trainings and, most importantly their instructors.  After such a trial of looking around for the best style and the best instructor, take your first step and sign up for several lessons, usually for a month.  Try to decide, during that month and not after, if it is good for you to continue with the chosen style and with the chosen place.

After you have decided to stay, you should listen and execute anything that your instructor says to you.  If you have difficulty in keeping up with a certain rhythm imposed by the instructor, don't be shy.  Discuss it with him after the lesson.  A good instructor usually listens and will change the regimen to your satisfaction.  If the instructor does not listen and will not try to change, you should not quit, instead you should go to another school more suitable for your physical and/or mental abilities.

However, keep in mind that, sometimes, the problem is not the school or the instructor, but it may be you and what kind of person you are.  You should understand, no matter how talented you are or good the school is, it is really a combination of that, together with your willingness and dedication to the art that is going to make a difference.

**Appendix B: Addresses**

• International Sendo-Ryu Karatedo Federation - 27-18 Newtown Ave., 3rd floor, Astoria NY 11102 - USA - WORLD - HOMBU, President and Founder, Prof. Emeric Arus, Ph.D./SOKE 10th Dan.

• German representative of Sendo-Ryu Karatedo - Maiwandstrasse 3. D- 83098 Brannenburg - Germany, Norbert W. Punzet/Shihan 7th Dan Kun-Tai-Ko Karate, 5th Dan Sendo-Ryu Karate.

• Hungarian Sendo-Ryu Karatedo Federation - Majus 1 utca 5 szam, ap:14 Zalaegerszeg - 8900 - Hungary, Dr. ing. Attila A. Czegeni/Shihan 6th Dan.

• Romanian Federation of Sendo-Ryu Karatedo - Com: Baciu Nr. 266, code: 407055, Jud: Cluj - Romania, Mrs. Emoke Bartis - 3rd Dan, Mr. ing. Cornel Hoza - 2nd Dan.

• Armenian Federation of Sendo-Ryu Karatedo - St. Roubinyants, apt.1, flat 57 Yerevan - Armenia, Mr. Aghvan Shahbazyan.

• India - President Sensei Lazman Sitaram Ziman - Email: krutikado@yahoo.co.in

**Notes to the Text**

(1)  This is best described as an attack into the opponent's attack.  It can be thought of as a stopping attack, when the opponent's attack cannot be finalized as one's own attack has been faster; although this can be understood as blocking and attacking into the opponent's attack. (p:6)

(2) Initiative in defense means creating openings that will lead your opponent to attack which, in turn, will enable you to know what he will come back with, therefore making it easy for you to counterattack. (p:6)

(3)  Range of motion refers to the movement of a specific joint.  This motion is influenced by several structures:  bony congruence, the joint capsule, ligaments, muscles and tendons acting on the joint.  The athlete executes a motion, which begins with the muscles and joint to be facilitated at a maximally stretched position and end with muscles and joint at the maximally shortened end of their range. (p:19)

(4) Normal endpoint at the shortened end in the range of motion (e.g. elbow in flexion position).  Normal endpoint at the maximally stretched position in the range of motion (e.g. elbow in full extension position). (p:19)

(5) Anaerobic means the exercises are done in the absence of oxygen (during isometric exercises the athlete stops breathing). (p:19)

(6) The part of the nervous system, comprising the brain and the spinal cord.  Has two fundamental functions:  a) Reflex function  b) Leading function. (p:58)

(7) The biceps muscles have more of a role in a pulling action, while the triceps muscles have more of a role in a pushing action. (p:62)

(8)  Advancing or moving forward. (p:84)

(9)  Process of turning on an axis. (p:84)

(10)  The lateral movement of the limbs away from median plane of the body. (p:84)

(11)  Movement of a limb toward median plane of body or toward axial line of a limb. (p:84)

(12)  The act of bending or condition of being bent in contrast to extension. (p:86)

(13)  The movement by which both ends of any part are pulled apart.  A movement that brings the limbs into or toward a straight condition. (p:86)

(14) Type of training whose main objective is the improvement of athlete's motor capacity, necessary to obtain high results, which is realized through different means characteristic of the speed, strength and endurance training, specific for each sport branch. (p:163)

(15) Overtraining is the athlete's pathological state in which he is negatively influencing his capacity of adaptation to effort, manifested particularly because of an irrational stress or effort in training. (p:164)

(16)  Refers to a rib and its cartilage. (p:174)

(17)  In the brain some exercises can help for a better learning (positive transfer) and other exercises can destroy the quality of learning (negative transfer). (p:179)

## About the author

Professor Emeric Arus was born in Romania on June 9, 1938. In 1970 he finished the "Institute of Physical Education and Sports" in Bucharest and earned a State Diploma as a Professor of Physical Education, specializing in Judo as a Judo Professor. As an Assistant College Professor in his native town, Professor Arus taught biomechanics, theory and methodology of sports, sports hygiene, sports history, weight lifting and Judo.

At the age of 13 he started practicing modern fencing, eventually acquiring two national championship titles in saber. In 1958 he obtained 6th place in the Junior World Fencing Championships in Bucharest, and in 1960 he obtained 6th place with the Romanian saber team at the Rome Olympic Games. He achieved many other leading positions in modern fencing at different international championships between 1958 and 1963. While not competing in fencing, he practiced track and field, boxing, wrestling and weight lifting.

In 1968 at the age of thirty Emeric Arus started practicing Karate in conjunction with Judo and later with Jujitsu and Aikido. In 1971 he founded Seikakukai Budo Club in Oradea where he managed and taught Karate, Judo, Aikido and Kobudo. As a Romanian Judo coach he had remarkable results producing many children and junior Romanian champions some of which have reached the Senior Romanian Olympic team obtaining excellent international results in this art. Prof. Arus best student many times national champion Steven Nagy obtained a 2nd place in the Junior Judo European Championships in 1984 and placed 5th in the Senior Judo World Championships in the following year.

Professor Arus never had any constant instructor in the Budo field, but he traveled extensively, accumulating knowledge and meeting several noted instructors in the Judo, Karate and Aikido fields. He trained for three years under the direction of master Hang Chiang Hi, 6th Dan Kodokan, a Korean master of Judo, trained under the direction of Juo Iwamoto 4th Dan, head of the Aikido Federation in Austria. Practiced Karate under the direction of Professor Roland Habersetzer 5th Dan Shotokan, Augusto Basile 6th Dan Wado-Ryu, Tatsuo Suzuki - Hanshi 8th Dan Wado-Ryu, head of the European Wado-Kai.

Professor Arus immigrated to the United States in 1981 where his martial arts expertise grew tremendously. He practiced Karate under many different American masters such as Cecile T. Patterson, 8th Dan Wado-Ryu, the late regretted Shotokan Karate master Frederick J. Hamilton. Practiced Aikijujutsu under the direction of Dr. George R. Parulski, Jr. 8th Dan Menkyo/Kaiden.

From 1984 to 1991, Professor Arus was head coach of fencing and Karate instructor at Brooklyn College in New York. After 1991 Professor Arus taught in various places throughout New York City, his students (especially juniors) obtained great results in Karate as well as in fencing.

On November 14, 1987 Professor Arus founded Sendo-Ryu Karatedo/The Way of Initiative style which has been recognized by: Dai Nippon Seibukan Budo Bugei Kai Japan, World Headfounders/Headfamilies Council, the United States Karate Association and the United States Martial Arts Association. Prof. Arus further succeeded in establishing Sendo-Ryu Karate clubs in Europe. In 1987 finished at Long Island University "The Karate Instructor Certificate Program" and in 1991 obtained a MS in Physical Education from Brooklyn College. Emeric Arus obtained a Ph.D. in Human Movement Science from Atlantic International University.

Prof. Arus has been inducted into the Hall of Fame in 1992 by World Headfounders/Headfamilies Council and on August 12, 2000 by the United States Martial Arts Association. He also obtained 9th Dan in Sendo-Ryu Karatedo and grandmaster status backed by the Supreme Grandmaster Fusei Kise from Okinawa. Emeric Arus has been promoted to 10th Dan by the World Headfounders/ Headfamilies Council in 2005. Presently Professor Arus has been appointed by the United States Martial Arts Association president, O-Sensei Philip S. Porter, as the Chairman of the Curriculum Development Committee for the University of Martial Arts and Sciences.

Professor Arus holds the following ranks in martial arts:
- 10th Dan Sendo-Ryu Karate
- 6th Dan Jujitsu
- 5th Dan Kindai-Ha Shito-Ryu Karate & Instructor Certificate
- 5th Dan Shotokan Karate
- 4th Dan Judo
- 3rd Dan Wado-Ryu Karate

## Bibliography

Burke R.Dennis, M.D., *Treating Martial Arts Injuries*. Ohara Publications, 1981.

Clark, Robert 9th Dan, *Master's Jiu Jitsu*. Pelham Books Ltd. England, 1988.

Corcoran, John and Farkas, Emil, *Martial Arts: Traditions, History, People*. Gallery Books, 1983.

Funakoshi, Gichin, *Karate-Do, My way of life*. Kodansha International Ltd., 1975

Habersetzer, Roland, *Guide Le Marabout du Karate: L'art du combat a mains nues*. Editions Gerard & C, Verviers (Belgique), 1969.

Habersetzer, Roland, *Le Karate Technique Wado-Ryu*. Flammarion-Paris, 1968.

Higaonna, Morio, *Traditional Karatedo - Vol.1*. Minato Research/Japan Publications, 1985.

Hisataka, Masayuki, *Scientific Karatedo: Spiritual Development of Individuality in Mind and Body*. Japan Publications Inc., 1976.

Leonard, C.H., AM., MD, *The Concise Gray's Anatomy*. Chartwell Book Inc., 1983.

Nakaya, Takao, *Karate-do History and Philosophy*. JSS Publishing Company, 1986.

Nakayama, Masatoshi, *Best Karate: 1 Comprehensive  2 Fundamentals  3 Kumite 1,* Kodansha International Ltd., 1977/1978.

Ohgami, Shingo, *Introduction to Karate*. Published by Japanska Magasinet, Goteborg, Sweden, 1984.

Palumbo G. Dennis, *The Secrets of Hakkoryu Jujutsu: Shodan Tactics*. Paladin Press, 1987.

Papilian, Victor, *Anatomia Omului: Vol I  Aparatul Locomotor*. Editura Didactica si Pedagogica, Bucuresti 1974, Edit. a V-a.

Prentice E. William Ph.D. A.T., C., P.T., *Rehabilitation Techniques in Sport Medicine*. Times Mirror/Mosby College Publishing, 1990.

Rabesa, Arthur, *Kumite: The Complete Fighting Text*. Peabody Publishing Co. Inc., 1984.

Ratti, Oscar/Westbrook, Adele, *Secrets of the Samurai*. Charles E. Tuttle Company, Inc., 1980.

Stevens, John, *Three Budo Masters*. Kodansha International Ltd., 1995

Teruyuki, Okazaki/Stricevic V. Milorad, M.D., *The Textbook of Modern Karate*. Kodansha International Ltd., 1984.

Theodorescu, Dem, *Mic Atlas de Anatomia Omului*. Editura Didactica si Pedagogica, Bucuresti, 1974.

Torg S. Joseph,  Joseph J. Vegso, Elisabeth, Torg, *Rehabilitation of Athletic Injuries: An Atlas of Therapeutic Exercise*. Year Book Medical Publishers Inc., 1987.

Ueshiba, Kisshomaru, *Aikido*. Hozansha Publications Co., Ltd., Tokyo, Japan, 1985.

Velte, Herbert, *Budo Lexicon: 1500 Fachausdrucke Fernostlicher Kampfsportarten*. Falken - Verlag Erich Sicher, 1976.

*** F.A. Davis Company - Philadelphia - Taber's Cyclopedic Medical Dictionary, 1989

*** Merriam - Webster - Springfield, MA 01102 - Webster's New Explorer Medical Dictionary,  Copyright © 1999 by Merriam - Webster, Incorporated.

*** The Journal of the American Medical Association, Vol 244, No. 5. Aug. 1.1980.

*** Torteneti Kronologia I. II. - Kriterion Konyvkiado Bukarest - 1976.

# Martial Arts Glossary

### Pronouncing Japanese words

Transcription of Japanese words in the Roman alphabet follows the rules of English phonetics.  Writing Japanese words using the Roman alphabet is called *Romanji.* Roman indicate the language origin and ji means word(s) in Japanese.

Here are several examples of Romanji and their pronunciation:

| | | |
|---|---|---|
| w - pronounced | = ua  or  wa | - wa (ua)  = harmony, accord |
| sh -         " | = shee | - shiho (sheehoh)  = four direction |
| chi -        " | = chee | - chikara (cheekarah)  = power |
| j -          " | = joo or djoo | - judo (djoodoh)  = gentle way |
| z -          " | = z  or  dz | - za (dza)  = seat |
| ts -         " | = tsk | - tsuki (tskee)  = thrust or punch |
| ge -         " | = gha  or  geh | - gedan (ghadawn)  = lower level |
| gi  -        " | = ghee | - gi (ghee)  = uniform etc... |

## A

| | | |
|---|---|---|
| Abara | = | Ribs |
| Age | = | Upward |
| Age Hiji Ate | = | Rising elbow strike |
| Ageru | = | To raise or lift something |
| Age Teisho Uchi | = | Upward palmheel strike |
| Age Uke | = | Rising block |
| Age Zuki | = | Rising punch |
| Ago | = | Chin |
| Ago Osh | = | Pushing someone's chin upward |
| Ago Uch | = | Strike to the chin |
| Agura | = | To sit cross-legged (with one's legs crossed in front) |
| Ago Zuki | = | Uppercut to the chin |
| Ai | = | To join, unify |
| Ai Gamae | = | Both opponents are in same position (left to left) |
| Aiki | = | United spirit (the principle of taking an opponent's spirit or willpower) |
| Aikido | = | The way of unifying the spirit (martial art, which emphasize on holding, locking the wrist of an opponent and throwing with that position) |
| Aiki Otoshi | = | Throwing an opponent backward over one's thigh (Aikido technique) |

| | | |
|---|---|---|
| Ai Uchi | = | Simultaneous attack (strike) |
| Aori | = | Blue |
| Arashi | = | Storm |
| Arigato | = | Thank you |
| Arigato Gozaimashita | = | Thank you very much |
| Ashi | = | Leg or foot |
| Ashi Barai (Harai) | = | Sweeping the opponent's leg (usually the front leg) with the one's foot |
| Ashibo Kake Uke | = | Leg-hooking block |
| Ashi Dori | = | Leg take-down |
| Ashi Nage | = | Foot throw |
| Ashi No Ura | = | The sole of the foot |
| Ashi Sabaki | = | Foot work, shifting |
| Ashi Uke | = | Leg block |
| Ashi Uke Waza | = | Leg blocking technique |
| Ashi Waza | = | Foot technique |
| Ashi Yubi | = | The big toe |
| Atama | = | Head |
| Ate | = | Striking, to strike |
| Atemi | = | Striking a vital point |
| Atemi Waza | = | Techniques for striking vital points |
| Ato Uchi | = | Delayed blow |

## B

| | | |
|---|---|---|
| Banzai | = | Shout "Hurrah" |
| Barai | = | Sweep |
| Bassai | = | "To penetrate a fortress" a Karate Kata |
| Beikoku | = | Rice country (the USA) |
| Beikoku Jin | = | An American |
| Bo | = | A wooden staff (usually 6 feet long, 182 cm) |
| Bogu | = | Protective equipment |
| Bogu Kumite | = | Sparring with armor |
| Bojutsu | = | Fighting art of the stick, wooden staff |
| Bokken | = | A wooden sword |
| Bu | = | Martial or military |
| Budo | = | Martial way |
| Budokan | = | A building in which martial arts are taught (in Tokyo) |
| Budokwai | = | A center of practicing martial arts in London |
| Bugei | = | Old style martial art |
| Buke | = | A military samurai family |
| Buki | = | Weapons |
| Bujin | = | Warrior |
| Bujutsu | = | The art of war or martial art |

| | | |
|---|---|---|
| Bunkai Kata | = | The applications of a Kata techniques with partners |
| Bushi | = | Warrior (from samurai family) |
| Bushido | = | The way of code of ethics of the samurai |

### C

| | | |
|---|---|---|
| Chiburi | = | Blood shaking |
| Chika Ma | = | Short range distance |
| Chikara | = | Strength |
| Chikara Kurabe | = | Power test/competition |
| Chimpan (Shimpan) | = | Referee or judge |
| Chinto | = | An Okinawan Karate Kata whose name is said to mean literally, "Fighting toward the east", Gichin Funakoshi, the father of modern Karate, changed the name of this Kata to Gankaku ("Crane on a rock") |
| Chishi | = | A heavy stone on a wooden handle (used for strengthening the arm) |
| Choku Zuki | = | A straight punch (usually executed in a natural position) |
| Chu | = | Middle |
| Chudan | = | Middle level (the area from the clavicle bone to the waist) |
| Chudan Gamae (Kamae) | = | A middle guard fighting position |
| Chuden | = | Middle level teaching |
| Chudan Uchi Uke | = | Middle body section inward block |
| Chudan Uchi Ude Uke | = | Middle body section inward forearm block |
| Chudan Soto Ude Uke | = | Middle body section outward forearm block |
| Chugaeri | = | A somersault (forward rolling breakfall in Judo) |

### D

| | | |
|---|---|---|
| Dachi | = | Position, stance |
| Dai | = | Large, great |
| Dai Nippon | = | Great Japan |
| Dai Sensei (O Sensei) | = | Great teacher (a polite title for a teacher of Japanese martial arts holding 10th degree black belt rank) |
| Dan | = | A black belt degree or rank - There are ten ranks as follows: Shodan - 1st degree; Nidan - 2nd degree; Sandan - 3rd degree; Yondan - 4th degree; Godan - 5th degree; Rokudan - 6th degree; Shichidan - 7th degree; Hachidan - 8th degree; Kudan - 9th degree; Judan - 10th degree |
| Daito Ryu | = | A classical martial art style (Aikijujutsu) |
| Danryoku | = | Elasticity |
| Dan Zuki | = | Consecutive punch |
| De | = | Advancing |
| De Ashi Harai (Barai) | = | Advanced foot sweep |

| | | |
|---|---|---|
| Deshi | = | Trainee |
| Do | = | Way, road, path or trunk of the body |
| Dogi | = | A practice uniform used for Budo (Karategi used for Karate practice) |
| Dojo | = | A training hall where a martial art is practiced.  Literally means "The place of the way" |
| Dojo Arashi | = | Dojo storming - challenging the grandmaster of a Dojo |
| Dojo Kun | = | The guiding maxims of a Dojo |
| Domo Arigato | = | Thank you |
| Dori (Tori) | = | Grip, hold, catch |
| Dosa | = | Movement, exercise |
| Doshu | = | The headmaster of style |

### E

| | | |
|---|---|---|
| Embusen | = | The performance line of a Kata |
| Empi or Enpi | = | The elbow |
| Empi Kata | = | It is known as Wanshu of the Tomari style |
| Eri | = | Collar |
| Empi Uchi | = | An elbow strike |

### F

| | | |
|---|---|---|
| Fudo Dachi | = | Immovable stance or diagonal straddle leg stance |
| Fukusin Shugo | = | A term used in competition signaling the corner judges to come together for a decision |
| Fumi | = | Step |
| Fumi Dashi | = | A step forward |
| Fumi Kiri | = | Cutting kick (usually executed with Sokuto) |
| Fumi Komi | = | Inside step, stepping in |
| Fumi Komi Geri | = | A stomping kick |
| Fusen Sho (Fusen Gachi) | = | Victory by default in a competition |

### G

| | | |
|---|---|---|
| Gaeshi (Kaeshi) | = | To counter with the same technique |
| Gake | = | Hook (a technique executed with the arm or leg) |
| Gaiwan | = | Outside forearm area |
| Gankaku | = | A Shotokan style Karate Kata, originally it was known as Chinto |
| Garami | = | Holding in a locked position |
| Gari | = | A reaping action performed by the leg |
| Gassho | = | A Buddhist type of bow, done with the palms together in front of the face |
| Gatame | = | Holding, pinning |

| | | |
|---|---|---|
| Gedan | = | Lower level area (usually under the belt) |
| Gedan Barai | = | Downward sweeping block |
| Gedan No Kamae | = | Lower level fighting position |
| Gedan Uchi Barai | = | Inside downward sweeping block |
| Gedan Uke | = | Downward block |
| Geiko | = | Exercise, training |
| Genkan | = | The front entrance of Dojo |
| Genkotsu | = | Clenched fist |
| Geri (Keri) | = | Kick |
| Geta | = | Wooden sandals |
| Getsu | = | Moon |
| Go | = | Five |
| Gohon Kumite | = | Five steps or five attacks sparring |
| Gohonme | = | Fifth |
| Goju Ryu | = | A Japanese style of Karate, literally means the "Hard-soft style" |
| Goju Shiho | = | A Shotokan style Kata also in Sendo-Ryu "Fifty four steps" |
| Gokyu | = | Fifth class, it is an intermediate level in Karate and beginner level in Judo |
| Go No Sen | = | High initiative in defense or taking the initiative later |
| Goshi (Koshi) | = | Hip |
| Goshin Jutsu | = | The art of self-defense |
| Gyaku | = | Reverse, opposite |
| Gyaku Hanmi | = | Two opponent facing each other in opposite postures |
| Gyaku Mawashi Geri | = | Reverse roundhouse kick |
| Gyaku Te Dori | = | Reverse hand holding or grip |
| Gyaku Zuki | = | Reverse punch |

## H

| | | |
|---|---|---|
| Hachi | = | Eight |
| Hachiji Dachi | = | A formal stance or natural stance |
| Hadaka | = | Nude, empty, free |
| Hadaka Jime | = | A free choke, strangle |
| Hai | = | Yes, all right |
| Haishu | = | The back of the hand |
| Haishu Uchi | = | A back hand strike |
| Haishu Uke | = | A back hand block |
| Haisoku | = | Instep |
| Haito | = | Ridge hand |
| Haito Uchi | = | A ridge hand strike |
| Haito Uke | = | A ridge hand block |
| Haiwan | = | The back part of the forearm |
| Hajime | = | To begin |

| | | |
|---|---|---|
| Hakama | = | A large skirt with two large part as pants worn by many traditional martial artists |
| Hakko Ryu | = | A style of Ju Jutsu in which Atemi techniques are emphasized |
| Han | = | Half |
| Handachi | = | Kneeling on one knee |
| Hangetsu Dachi | = | Half moon stance |
| Hangetsu Kata | = | Literally means "Half Moon" it is known also as Seishan |
| Hanmi | = | The torso is twisted 45 degrees angle towards the opponent |
| Hanshi | = | An honorary title, master of masters, between 8th and 10th Dan |
| Hansoku | = | Foul, losing a contest by fault |
| Hantei | = | A decision call (in a competition) |
| Hara Gatame | = | An armlock which locks the opponent's elbow on the defender's stomach |
| Hara Kiri | = | Stomach cut also known as Seppuku |
| Hasami Uchi | = | Scissors strike |
| Hasami Zuki | = | Scissors punch |
| Hayai | = | Fast |
| Heian Kata | = | A series of five Karate Kata also known as Pinan, literally means "Peaceful mind" |
| Heiho | = | Strategy |
| Hombu Dojo | = | The central (main) Dojo of an organization |
| Honryu | = | The main style |

## I

| | | |
|---|---|---|
| Iai | = | Sword exercise |
| Iaido | = | Way of the sword |
| Iai Jutsu | = | The art of sword drawing |
| Iaito | = | A sword used for Iaido, not an original |
| Ibuki | = | A breathing method featuring a long exhalation, followed by a short cough to expel the last of the air |
| Ichi | = | One |
| Ichi Ryu | = | First class |
| Idori | = | Seated defense |
| Iie | = | No |
| Ikken Hisatsu | = | One punch kills the demon, one punch death blow |
| Ikkyu | = | First class or level - of the advanced, this is before the 1st Dan black belt level |
| Ima | = | Now |
| Ippon | = | One point |
| Ippon Ken | = | One knuckle fist |
| Ippon Kumite | = | One step sparring or one attack sparring |
| Ipponme | = | The first |
| Ippon Nukite | = | One finger spear hand |

| | | |
|---|---|---|
| Ippon Seoi nage | = | One arm shoulder throw |
| Ippon Shobu | = | One point match |
| Irimi | = | An execution of entering to your opponent |
| Iro Obi | = | In Karate a colored belt |

## J

| | | |
|---|---|---|
| Jigo or Jigotai | = | Defensive |
| Jigo Hontai | = | Defensive position, this position is lower than Shizentai position |
| Jikan | = | "Time", a term used by timekeeper at the end of a Karate or Judo match |
| Jintai | = | Body |
| Jintai Kyusho | = | The vital points of the human body |
| Jion | = | Karate Kata, a name of a Buddhist temple in China |
| Jitsu | = | Reality, truth, technique, |
| Jiu (Ju) | = | Gentle, mild, soft |
| Jiu Jitsu | = | Soft technique |
| Jiyu | = | Free |
| Jiyu Ippon Kumite | = | Free sparring with one technique |
| Jiyu Kumite | = | Free sparring |
| Jo | = | Upper, a 120 cm long staff |
| Jodan | = | Upper level |
| Jodan Uke | = | Upper level block |
| Jodan Gamae (Kamae) | = | Upper level fighting position |
| Jogai (Jogai Nakae) | = | Out of contest area |
| Joseki | = | "Upper side" where instructors stay in a Dojo |
| Joshu | = | Assistant |
| Josokutei (Koshi) | = | Ball of the foot |
| Ju | = | Ten, soft |
| Judo | = | "The gentle way" |
| Judoka | = | A Judo practitioner |
| Juji | = | Cross |
| Juji Gatame | = | Cross armlock |
| Juji Jime | = | Cross choke |
| Juji Nage | = | A throw by holding the opponent arms in a crossed position |
| Juji Uke | = | Cross block |
| Jutsu | = | Art, science |
| Jujutsu | = | Soft art |
| Jumbi Taiso (Jumbi Undo) | = | Warm-up exercises |
| Jun Geri | = | A kick with front leg |
| Jupponme | = | Tenth |
| Jushin (Itten) | = | Center of gravity |
| Jutte | = | A Karate Kata literally means "Ten hands" |
| Jun Zuki | = | A lunge punch or stepping punch |

| | | |
|---|---|---|
| Ju Yoku Go O Sei Suru | = | Old Jujutsu maxim, "Softness controls hardness" |

## K

| | | |
|---|---|---|
| Kachi (Gachi) | = | Victory or win |
| Kagi | = | Hook (technique executed only with the arm) |
| Kagi Zuki | = | Hook punch |
| Kai | = | A suffix denoting an organization or a club (e.g., Jukokai, Wadokai, Kyokushinkai etc.) |
| Kaicho | = | President, the head of a federation, association |
| Kaiden Shihan | = | Master appointed title from the Soke of the style |
| Kaisho | = | Open hand |
| Kaiten | = | Rotation, turning |
| Kaiten Nage | = | A rotation throwing, an Aikido technique |
| Kakato | = | Heel of the foot |
| Kakato Geri | = | Heel kick |
| Kakato Otoshi | = | Heel drop |
| Kake Uke | = | Hook block |
| Kakuto | = | Bent wrist |
| Kama | = | Sicle |
| Kamae | = | Fighting position |
| Kamaete | = | Taking the position before a Karate match |
| Kancho | = | Director or master of the style |
| Kanku Dai | = | A Karate Kata, literally means "Looking at the sky" early name known as Kusanku or Kushanku |
| Kansetsu Geri | = | Joint kick (usually executed against the knee articulation with a stamping motion) |
| Kansetsu Waza | = | Joint locking techniques |
| Kappo or Kuatsu | = | Japanese resuscitation system |
| Kara | = | Empty |
| Karate | = | Empty hand |
| Karate Do | = | "The way of empty hand" |
| Karategi | = | Karate uniform |
| Karateka | = | Karate practitioner |
| Karate Ni Sente Nashi | = | Funakoshi's maxim, which states "Never attack first in Karate" |
| Kasumi | = | Feint, haze |
| Kata | = | Shoulder, formal exercise |
| Kata Hiza | = | Kneeling on one knee |
| Katame Waza (Ne Waza) | = | Grappling (ground) techniques in Judo which consist of: Osae Waza, Kansetsu Waza and Shime Waza |
| Katana | = | Sword |
| Katate | = | One handed grab |
| Kawashi | = | Dodging |
| Keage | = | Snap (snap kick) |

| | | |
|---|---|---|
| Keiko (Geiko) | = | Exercise |
| Keikogi | = | Practice uniform |
| Keito | = | Chiken head wrist |
| Kekomi | = | Thrust (thrust kick) |
| Ken | = | Fist, sword, hard |
| Kendo | = | "The way of the sword" |
| Kenpo (Kempo) | = | Fist way or fist method |
| Kentsui (Tettsui) | = | Hammer fist |
| Kentsui Hasami Uchi | = | Double hammer fist (executed in a scissor motion) |
| Kentsui Uchi | = | Hammer fist strike |
| Ki | = | Spirit |
| Kiai | = | "Meeting of the spirit", a yelling act in connection with the expulsion of air |
| Kiba Dachi | = | Straddle-leg stance or horse riding stance |
| Kihon | = | Basic, in Karate is the repetitions of the basic techniques |
| Kihon Kata Kumite | = | Basic formal sparring |
| Kihon Kumite | = | Basic sparring |
| Kime | = | Focus |
| Kimono | = | A Japanese robe |
| Ki Nagare | = | Energy flow |
| Kin Geri | = | A Karate kick to the groin using the instep |
| Kiri | = | Cut |
| Kiri Age | = | Cut upward |
| Kiri Otoshi | = | Cutting downward |
| Kiritsu | = | Stand up |
| Kiso | = | Fundamentals |
| Ko | = | Small |
| Kobudo | = | Weapons way, the practice of Okinawan weaponry, which include the staff (Bo), sicle (Kama), pronged truncheon (Sai), handle (Tonfa), flail (Nunchaku) and weighted chain (Manriki Gusari) |
| Kobushi Uchi | = | Fist strike |
| Kodokan | = | The famous Judo institute in Tokyo |
| Kohai | = | Junior student |
| Kokoro | = | Spirit, heart |
| Kokutsu Dachi | = | Back stance |
| Kokyu | = | Respiration |
| Komi | = | Inside |
| Konban Wa | = | Good evening |
| Konnichi Wa | = | Good afternoon |
| Kosa Dachi | = | Cross-legged stance |
| Koshi Waza | = | Hip techniques |
| Kote | = | The wrist or the lower part of the forearm |
| Kote Uchi | = | Strike with the wrist |

| | | |
|---|---|---|
| Ko Uchi Gari | = | Small inner-reap |
| Ku | = | Nine |
| Kubi | = | Neck |
| Kumade | = | Bear hand |
| Kuzure | = | Variant |
| Kuzushi | = | Off balancing |
| Kyoshi | = | A master instructor, the bearer must be at least 6th or 7th degree black belt rank |
| Kyotsuke | = | Attention |
| Kyu | = | Mudansha class, not black belt class |
| Kyucho | = | The senior Mudansha in Dojo |
| Kyusho | = | A vital point on the body |

## M

| | | |
|---|---|---|
| Ma | = | Distance, straight |
| Ma Ai | = | Distancing |
| Mae Ashi Geri | = | Front leg kick |
| Mae Empi Uchi | = | Front elbow strike |
| Mae Geri | = | Front kick |
| Mae Hiza Geri | = | Front knee kick |
| Mae Tobi Geri | = | Flying front kick, jumping front kick |
| Mae Ukemi | = | A forward break-fall |
| Maki | = | Roll, turn, twist |
| Maki Komi | = | Roll inside |
| Makiwara | = | Punching board, made of hard wood and padded with bundled straw or hard rubber |
| Mata | = | Thigh |
| Matte | = | Stop |
| Maware | = | Turn around |
| Mawashi | = | Round, rotation |
| Mawashi Geri | = | Roundhouse kick |
| Mawashi Uke | = | Roundhouse block |
| Mawashi Zuki | = | Roundhouse punch |
| Mawatte | = | Turn |
| Meijin | = | A supreme master, genius |
| Men | = | The face |
| Menjo | = | Diploma or certificate of rank |
| Menkyo | = | A Yudansha rank certificate |
| Menkyo Kaiden | = | A teacher's certificate in a certain Ryu |
| Men Uchi | = | Strike to the face |
| Migi | = | Right (direction) |
| Migi Ato Sumi | = | Right rear corner |
| Migi Naname Mae | = | Diagonally right front |

| | | |
|---|---|---|
| Migi Naname Ushiro | = | Diagonally right back |
| Migi Yoko | = | Right side |
| Mikazuki | = | Crescent moon |
| Mikazuki Geri | = | Crescent kick |
| Mizu | = | Water |
| Mizu No Kokoro | = | A mind like a water (calm) |
| Mochi | = | Grip |
| Mochi Age | = | To lift up |
| Mokuroku | = | A certificate of lower level |
| Mokuso | = | Meditation |
| Morote | = | With both hands |
| Morote Dori | = | Holding or grappling with both hands the opponent's wrists |
| Morote Gari | = | Scooping up the opponent both legs from the front |
| Morote Teisho | = | Both palm heels |
| Morote Tsukami Uke | = | Two-handed grasping block |
| Morote Uke | = | Augmented forearm block |
| Morote Zuki | = | Both hands punch |
| Mune | = | Chest |
| Mudansha | = | A white or colored belt student, not a black belt student |
| Musubi Dachi | = | Informal attention stance |

## N

| | | |
|---|---|---|
| Nagai | = | Long |
| Nagashi | = | Flowing |
| Nagashi Mawashi Zuki | = | Flowing round punch |
| Nagashi Zuki | = | Flowing punch |
| Nagashi Uke | = | Flowing or sweeping block |
| Nage | = | Throw |
| Naihanchi (Naifanchi) | = | Okinawan Karate Kata, in Sendo-Ryu Karate now is called Tekki |
| Naiwan | = | Inside forearm (the ulna bone part) |
| Naka | = | Center |
| Nakadaka Ipponken | = | Middle finger knuckle fist |
| Nakayubi | = | Middle finger |
| Nami | = | Wave |
| Nami Gaeshi or Nami Ashi | = | Inward snapping foot hook |
| Naname | = | Diagonal |
| Neko Ashi Dachi | = | Cat foot stance |
| Ne Waza | = | Ground techniques |
| Ni | = | Two |
| Nidai | = | Second generation |
| Nidan Geri | = | Double front snap kick - executed to two level |
| Nihonme | = | Second |

| | | |
|---|---|---|
| Nihon Nukite | = | Two finger spear hand |
| Nihon Zuki | = | Double punch |
| Nijushiho | = | Karate Kata "24 directions" |
| Nippon | = | Japan |
| Nogare | = | A breathing method |
| Nukite | = | Spear hand |

## O

| | | |
|---|---|---|
| O | = | Big, large, major, great, God |
| Obi | = | Belt |
| Aka Obi | = | Red belt |
| Aori Obi | = | Blue belt |
| Chairo Obi | = | Brown belt |
| Daidaiiro Obi | = | Orange belt |
| Kiiro Obi | = | Yellow belt |
| Kuro Obi | = | Black belt |
| Midori Obi | = | Green belt |
| Shiro Obi | = | White belt |
| Ohayo Gozaimasu | = | Good morning, before 10 A.M. |
| Okinawa Te | = | Okinawa hand, the old name of Karate |
| Okuri | = | Both |
| Oi | = | Non reverse position or form |
| Oi Zuki (Jun Zuki) | = | Lunge punch |
| Omote | = | The front |
| Os, Oss, Osu | = | Yes, (I understand, I am ready to do) |
| Osae | = | Pinning |
| Osae Waza | = | Pinning techniques |
| Osaeru | = | Hold down |
| O Sensei | = | A great teacher |
| Oshi | = | Push |
| O Soto Gari | = | Large outer-reap, Judo technique |
| Otagai Ni Rei | = | Bow to each other |
| Otoshi | = | Dropping an arm or leg |
| Otoshi Empi Uchi | = | Downward elbow strike |
| O Uchi Gari | = | Large inner-reap |
| Oyasumi Nasai | = | Good night |

## R

| | | |
|---|---|---|
| Randori | = | Free style sparring  (in Judo) |
| Rei | = | A command to bow |
| Rengeri | = | Double front kick (one after one) |

| Renmei (Remmei) | = | Federation |
| Renoji Dachi | = | Natural stance or "L" stance |
| Renraku Waza | = | Combination techniques by repeating different techniques |
| Renshi | = | A 4th or a 5th Dan black belt teacher |
| Renzoku | = | Combination by repeating same techniques |
| Ri Ai | = | Rhythm |
| Ritsurei | = | Standing bow |
| Roku | = | Six |
| Ropponme | = | Sixth |
| Ryo | = | Meaning both (legs or arms) |
| Ryo Ashi | = | Both feet, legs |
| Ryo Te | = | Both hands |
| Ryote Dori | = | Holding an opponent's arm with both hands |

## S

| Sabaki | = | Turning |
| Sagi Ashi Dachi | = | One-legged stance |
| Sai | = | Trident shaped weapon |
| Samurai | = | Warrior, a servant to the lord |
| San | = | Three or Mr. |
| Sanbon | = | Third |
| Sanbon Kumite | = | Three steps sparring, three attacks sparring |
| Sanbon Zuki | = | Triple punch |
| Sanchin | = | An Okinawan Karate Kata, hourglass |
| Sanchin Dachi | = | Hourglass stance |
| Sandai | = | Third generation |
| Sankaku (Sangaku) | = | Triangle |
| Sankaku Jime | = | Triangular choking |
| Sanren Zuki | = | Three consecutive punches |
| Saya | = | Scabbard of a sword |
| Satori | = | Enlightenment |
| Seiken | = | Forefist (palm parts downwards) |
| Seiryoku Zenyo | = | Make the best use of energy |
| Seiryuto | = | Ox jaw hand |
| Seishan | = | An Okinawan Karate Kata also known as Hangetsu |
| Seishan Dachi | = | Fighting position in Sendo-Ryu Karate style |
| Seitei | = | Standard |
| Seiza | = | A kneeling - seated position |
| Sempai | = | Senior student |
| Sen | = | Initiative |
| Sen No Sen | = | Earlier initiative (an attack in the opponent's attack) |
| Sensei | = | Teacher |

| | | |
|---|---|---|
| Seoi | = | Back of the body |
| Seppuku | = | Suicide executed with knife on the abdomen |
| Shi | = | Four |
| Shiai | = | Contest |
| Shichi | = | Seven |
| Shihan | = | Master, from sixth degree black belt and up |
| Shiaijo | = | Contest area |
| Shiho | = | Four directions |
| Shiken | = | Examination |
| Shikko | = | Walking on the knees, practiced in Aikido |
| Shiko Dachi | = | Squat stance or Sumo stance |
| Shime | = | Choking or strangulation |
| Shimoseki or Shimoza | = | Lower seat in Dojo (left side seat) |
| Shimpan | = | Referee |
| Shin | = | Mind, new |
| Shinai | = | A sword made of bamboo strips |
| Shinken | = | Real sword |
| Shinken Shobu | = | Fight to the death |
| Shintai | = | Normal walking forward or backward |
| Shisei | = | Stance or posture |
| Shita | = | Down |
| Shita Hara | = | Lower abdomen |
| Shizentai | = | Natural stance |
| Shobu Ippon | = | Contest for one full point |
| Shochu Geiko | = | Summer training |
| Shodai | = | First generation |
| Shomen | = | Front |
| Shotei (Teisho) | = | Palm-heel |
| Shotei Osae | = | Palm-heel press |
| Shotei Otoshi Uke | = | Dropping palm-heel block |
| Shotei Uchi | = | Palm-heel strike |
| Shotei Zuki | = | Palm-heel thrust |
| Shotokan | = | Japanese Karate style, the most popular in the world today its founder was Gichin Funakoshi. Funakoshi's penname was Shoto and Kan means school |
| Shuto or Tegatana | = | Knife hand |
| Shuto Uchi | = | Knife hand strike |
| Shuto Uke | = | Knife hand block |
| Sochin Dachi | = | Diagonal straddle-leg stance also known as Fudo Dachi |
| Sode Dori (Tori) | = | Hold on sleeve |
| Sokumen | = | Side |
| Sokutei (Teisoku) | = | Sole of the foot |
| Sokuto | = | Sword foot or foot edge |
| Sono Mama | = | "Don't move" a Judo contest term, means stay still |

| | | |
|---|---|---|
| Sore Made | = | "That is all", means end of a match, contest |
| Soto | = | Exterior, outside |
| Soto Uke | = | Outside block |
| Sukui | = | Scoop up |
| Sukui Nage | = | Scooping throw |
| Sukui Uke | = | Scooping block |
| Sumi | = | Corner |
| Sumi Gaeshi | = | Corner throw (turn) |
| Sumi Otoshi | = | Corner drop |
| Sumo | = | Japanese wrestling |
| Suri Ashi | = | Gliding step |
| Sutemi | = | Sacrifice |

## T

| | | |
|---|---|---|
| Tachi | = | Stand |
| Tachi Waza | = | Standing techniques |
| Tai | = | Body |
| Taido | = | Old name for Jujutsu |
| Taikai | = | Demonstration |
| Taikyoku | = | The most basic Kata in Karate |
| Tai Sabaki | = | Body turning by shifting |
| Taiso | = | Warm-up exercises |
| Tameshiwari | = | Breaking test |
| Tanbo (Tambo) | = | A club or short stick |
| Tanden | = | Abdomen, stomach |
| Tanto | = | Dagger, the blade approximately is 8-9 inches long |
| Tanto Dori | = | Taking the knife away from an opponent |
| Tashi (Tasshi) | = | Expert |
| Tatami | = | Special mats, made of bundled straw |
| Tate | = | Vertical |
| Tate Empi Uchi | = | Upward elbow strike |
| Tateken | = | Vertical fist |
| Te | = | Hand |
| Teiji Dachi | = | "T" stance |
| Teisho | = | Palm-heel |
| Tekubi | = | Wrist |
| Te Nagashi Uke | = | Sweeping hand block |
| Tenkan | = | Turn, reverse |
| Te Osae Uke | = | Pressing hand block |
| Tetsu | = | Iron |
| Tetsu Geta | = | Iron slipper |
| Tettsui (Kentsui) | = | Hammer-fist |

| | | |
|---|---|---|
| Tettsui Uchi | = | Hammer-fist strike |
| Te Ude Uke Waza | = | Hand, arm blocking techniques |
| Te Waza | = | Hand techniques |
| Tobi | = | Jump |
| Tobi Komi | = | Jump forward |
| Tobi Komi Zuki | = | Jumping punch or jab |
| Tode | = | Old name for Karate in Okinawa |
| To Ma (Toma) | = | Large distance for fighting - usually need a step to reach the opponent |
| Tonfa | = | Handle, a Karate weapon |
| Tori | = | A person who execute a technique first, attacker (grab, kick, punch, throw etc) |
| Tsuba | = | The guard of a samurai sword |
| Tsuri | = | Pull |
| Tsugi | = | Succession |
| Tsugi Ashi | = | Sliding step |
| Tsuka | = | Handle of a sword |
| Tsukami | = | Grab |
| Tsuki | = | Moon, thrust |
| Tsuki No Kokoro | = | "A mind like a moon", so clear |
| Tsuki Uke | = | Blocking with thrust into opponent's attack |
| Tsukuri | = | Preparatory action after off-balancing has been made in Judo |
| Tsumasaki | = | Tips of the toes |
| Tsuzukete | = | Continue |

## U

| | | |
|---|---|---|
| Uchi | = | Strike, inside, inward |
| Uchi Deshi | = | Special apprentice, direct student of the master |
| Uchihachiji Dachi | = | Inverted open-leg stance |
| Uchi Komi | = | A preparatory and off-balancing action without throwing an opponent in Judo |
| Uchi Ma | = | Medium range distance |
| Uchi Shuto Uchi | = | Inward knife hand strike |
| Uchi Shuto Uke | = | Inward knife hand block |
| Uchi Sukui Uke | = | Inward scooping block |
| Uchi Teisho Uchi | = | Inward palm-heel strike |
| Uchi Ude Uke | = | Inward forearm block |
| Ude | = | Forearm |
| Ude Uke | = | Forearm block |
| Ue | = | Upper part |
| Uechi Ryu | = | Okinawan Karate style, founder Kanbum Uechi |
| Uke | = | Block, an opponent who executes a blocking technique or who is thrown by the opponent |

| | | |
|---|---|---|
| Ukemi | = | Falling, break-fall |
| Undo | = | Exercise |
| Ura | = | Reverse, opposite |
| Uraken (Riken) | = | Back fist |
| Uraken Uchi | = | Back fist strike |
| Ura Zuki | = | Close punch, uppercut |
| Ushiro | = | Back, rear, backward |
| Ushiro Empi Uchi | = | Elbow strike backward |
| Ushiro Geri | = | Back kick |
| Ushiro Kaiten | = | Backward turning or rotate |
| Ushiro Mawashi Geri | = | Back roundhouse kick |

## W

| | | |
|---|---|---|
| Wa | = | Peace, circular, harmony |
| Wado-Ryu | = | The way of peace school (style), founder Hironori Otsuka |
| Waka Sensei | = | The son of the headmaster of style |
| Wakarimasen | = | I don't understand |
| Wakarimasu | = | I understand |
| Waki | = | Armpit |
| Wanshu | = | Okinawan Karate Kata, known as Empi in Sendo-Ryu style |
| Washide | = | Eagle hand |
| Waza | = | Technique |
| Waza Ari (Waza Arri) | = | Half point in a tournament |

## Y

| | | |
|---|---|---|
| Yaku Soku Geiko | = | Prearranged practice |
| Yaku Soku Kumite | = | Prearranged sparring |
| Yama | = | Mountain |
| Yama Zuki | = | "U" punch |
| Yame | = | Stop |
| Yasume (Yasme) | = | Rest |
| Yoi | = | Ready or to be ready |
| Yoko | = | Side, lateral |
| Yoko Empi Uchi | = | Elbow strike laterally |
| Yoko Geri | = | Side kick |
| Yoko Geri Keage | = | Side-snap kick |
| Yoko Geri Kekomi | = | Side-thrust kick |
| Yokomen (Yoko Men) | = | Side of the body |
| Yokomen Uchi | = | Strike to the side |
| Yoko Tobi Geri | = | Jumping side kick |

| | | |
|---|---|---|
| Yoko Ukemi | = | Sideward break-fall |
| Yonhonme | = | Forth |
| Yonhon Nukite | = | Four finger spear-hand |
| Yoshi | = | Continue |
| Yubi | = | Finger |
| Yubi Hasami | = | Pinching |
| Yudansha | = | Black belt holder |
| Yusei Gachi (Kachi) | = | Win by superiority |

## Z

| | | |
|---|---|---|
| Za | = | Seat |
| Zanshin | = | Spirit alert, perfect finish |
| Zarei | = | Seated bow |
| Zazen | = | Sitting in Japanese style |
| Zen | = | All, sect of Buddhism |
| Zenkutsu Dachi | = | Front stance |
| Zenpo (Zempo) | = | Forward |
| Zenpo Kaiten | = | Forward roll |
| Zenpo Ukemi | = | Forward break-fall |
| Zori | = | Sandals |
| Zubon | = | Pants |
| Zuki (Tsuki) | = | Thrust, punch |

## Index

### A

absorbed blocks  77
Agura  15-16
Alexander the Great  3
Arakaki  5
art of Karatedo  7

### B

ballistic stretching  19
Bodhidharma  4
body rotation power  10, 63
body shifting  41
body vibration  63
breathing  13
Boxer Insurrection  4

### C

center of gravity  10
Ch'en Yuan Yun  4
Ch'ing dynasty  4
competitional  162-163-164

### D

distance  13-14
Dojo  8

### E

Egyptian tombs  3
evasion  49

### F

Funakoshi, Gichin  5, 75
focused blocks  75

### G

Goju-Ryu  5

### H

Hanagusuku, Nagashige  5
Hara  10
hard blocks  78
Higaonna, Kanryo  5
hip vibration  63
hooking  78

### I

Ibuki  29
I-Chin-Ching  4
Itosu, Yasutsune  5

### J

Jiyu-Kumite  7-8

### K

Kakuteijitsu  4
Karate schools/styles  5
Kata  7
Kempo/Kenpo  4
Ki  15
Kiai  7, 13
Kihon  7, 30
Kihon Dachi  33, 35
Kihon Kata Kumite  7
Kime  11-12
Kumite  7

### M

Mabuni, Kenwa  5
Makiwara  7, 9